Religion as a Mind Painting
Allen Schery

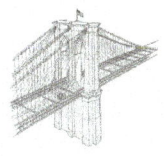

Brooklyn Bridge Books

Copyright ©2025 by Allen Schery

All rights reserved.

No portion of this book may be reproduced in any form without written permission from the publisher or author, except as permitted by U.S. copyright law.

Contents

Introduction The Unseen Threads of Belief		V
1. The Human Need for Narrative and the Birth of Myth		1
2. Defining Religion Across Cultures		14
3. Cognitive and Social Mechanisms		24
4. Creation Myths and Cosmologies		37
5. Miracles, Revelation, and Authority		50
6. Morality Without the Divine		63
7. Afterlife and Transcendence		76
8. Institutions, Power, and Social Control		89
9. Violence, Conflict, and Boundary-Making		103
10. Primate Power Dynamics — The WIIFM Machine		118
11. Religion as Cultural Heritage		132
12. Phenomenology of Meaning		146
13. Secular Humanism and Its Discontents		159
14. New Spiritualities and Hybrid Forms		171
15. Engineering Attack-Proof Coalitions in a Savanna-Shaped World		183

About the Author	193
Bibliography	197
Index	231
Endnotes	241

Introduction: The Unseen Threads of Belief

Why now? Because religion remains the most explosive force in human history—shaping empires, fueling conflicts, and embedding itself so deeply in our lives that we rarely pause to question its origins or long-held certainties. From the dawn of civilization to today's headlines, faith wields power over billions, yet beneath its veneer lies a remarkable paradox: religion is a human-constructed illusion, woven from stories we inherit long before we develop the critical distance to examine them.

We are born into narratives that define our world and bind us to our tribe. Long before we grasp logic or evidence, we absorb worldview-shaping myths as natural truth—a process I call narrative inheritance. Evolution has equipped us with sentinel awareness, an African-savanna–derived bias that spotlights threats within our group and filters out dissonant information, ensuring we remain loyal to the stories that sustain social cohesion. At the same time, our primate heritage reveals an opportunistic and amoral drive: we adopt and wield beliefs to gain advantage, unconstrained by intrinsic moral programming.

This book anticipates—and defends against—the inevitable philosophical objections. We employ methodological atheism, not as a covert materialist agenda, but as a neutral analytic stance that brackets truth claims to illuminate religion's human mechanics. Throughout, I maintain scholarly integrity by reflecting on my own insider/outsider positionality and acknowledging the limits of universal definitions.

Drawing on anthropology, sociology, psychology, history, philosophy, neuroscience, post-secular thought, and decolonial critique, The Grand Illusion offers a rigorous, cross-disciplinary journey. Readers will encounter critical inquiry fortified at every turn, robust defenses of our arguments, and a clear reckoning with the biases that have kept these illusions firmly in place. Prepare for a thorough, unflinching re-evaluation of religion's unseen threads—and for the explosive insights that follow.

Chapter One
The Human Need for Narrative and the Birth of Myth

Humans are storytelling animals by evolutionary design, wired for narrative construction long before we developed the critical apparatus to examine the stories themselves. This fundamental propensity emerges from our deep cognitive architecture—pattern recognition systems that evolved to detect threats, opportunities, and social alliances on African savannas millions of years ago. These same mechanisms that once helped our ancestors survive predators and navigate tribal dynamics now compel us to weave coherent explanations from fragments of experience, creating the mythic frameworks that become religious belief systems. The birth of myth represents not divine revelation or cultural accident, but the inevitable result of brains that must make meaning from uncertainty, brains that prioritize tribal cohesion over truth, and brains that adopt beliefs opportunistically based on social advantage rather than evidence.

To understand how religious myths emerge and persist, we must first acknowledge the cognitive biases that make myth-making inevitable. Pattern recognition—what neuroscientists describe as our brain's capacity to match environmental stimuli with stored memories—serves as the foundation for both survival and storytelling. Our ancestors who could quickly identify animal tracks, predict seasonal changes, or recognize facial expressions of danger survived to reproduce, passing on hyperactive pattern-detection systems that now see agency where none exists, design where randomness reigns, and purpose where only cause-and-effect unfolds. These same neural networks that once spotted camouflaged predators now construct elaborate creation stories to explain cosmic origins, miracle narratives to account for unlikely events, and afterlife beliefs to resolve mortality's uncomfortable randomness.

Contemporary cognitive science reveals that humans possess what researchers term "superior pattern processing" as the fundamental basis of our evolved brain architecture. This capacity enables us to excel at recognizing faces in crowds, understanding spoken language, and solving complex puzzles—abilities that require detecting meaningful relationships within seemingly chaotic information. However, this evolutionary advantage carries a mythogenic cost: our brains are so thoroughly adapted for pattern detection that they routinely identify patterns where none exist, a phenomenon psychologists call pareidolia. We see faces in clouds, divine messages in natural disasters, and moral purposes in random suffering because our neural architecture evolved to err on the side of false positives rather than miss genuine patterns that might prove fatal. Religious myths emerge as inevitable byproducts of this cognitive predisposition, transforming random environmental stimuli into elaborate supernatural narratives.

The mythmaking process operates through what evolutionary psychologists identify as confirmation bias—our tendency to seek, interpret, and remember information that confirms existing beliefs while dismissing contradictory evidence. Rather than representing a cognitive flaw, confirmation bias likely served crucial adaptive functions for our ancestors. In environments where quick decision-making meant survival, the ability to rapidly categorize new information based on existing templates provided decisive advantages. If previous encounters with certain animal tracks predicted danger, confirmation bias ensured our ancestors would interpret similar tracks as threats rather than waste precious time reconsidering past lessons. However, this same mechanism now operates to reinforce religious beliefs: believers selectively attend to confirmatory experiences (answered prayers, meaningful coincidences, moral victories) while filtering out disconfirming evidence (unanswered prayers, random tragedy, moral failures by co-believers).

Critics might argue that characterizing confirmation bias as an evolutionary adaptation oversimplifies its operation in contemporary religious contexts. They would correctly note that not all confirmation bias serves survival functions—some instances reflect motivated reasoning or social conformity rather than adaptive pattern recognition. This critique demands careful distinction between descriptive evolutionary accounts and normative evaluations of contemporary belief formation. When I describe confirmation bias as evolutionarily adaptive, I do not morally endorse its operation in modern religious contexts, but rather explain its persistence as a byproduct of neural systems that once provided survival advantages. The tendency to seek confirmatory evidence made evolutionary sense when environmental patterns remained relatively stable across generations. Religious believers today inherit these same neural predispositions, applying ancient pattern-recognition algorithms to metaphysical questions that lie far beyond their original adaptive domain.

The social dimension of confirmation bias reveals its function in what I term tribal cohesion. Recent research demonstrates that confirmation bias operates not merely as individual psychology but as group-level phenomenon that enhances collective decision-making through division of cognitive labor. When group members develop different initial hypotheses about environmental challenges, confirmation bias ensures that individuals pursue different investigative strategies, potentially maximizing the group's overall information-gathering capacity. Applied to religious contexts, this means that confirmation bias serves to maintain tribal unity by ensuring that community members continue supporting shared sacred narratives despite individual doubts or contradictory experiences. Religious communities that successfully cultivate confirmation bias create more psychologically committed members, stronger group boundaries, and more effective resistance to outside influence.

The opportunistic adoption of religious narratives reflects what I call the primate principle—the recognition that humans, like our closest evolutionary relatives, pursue social advantage without intrinsic moral constraints. Ethnographic evidence from countless societies reveals that individuals routinely adjust their religious commitments based on pragmatic considerations: social status, economic opportunity, political alliance, and personal crisis all influence belief adoption patterns more powerfully than theological arguments or mystical experiences. This opportunistic flexibility represents an evolutionary inheritance from ancestors who survived by forming advantageous coalitions, switching allegiances when necessary, and adopting whatever cultural practices enhanced their reproductive success. Contemporary believers inherit these same strategic tendencies, unconsciously calibrating their religious expressions to maximize social benefits within their particular cultural context.

The philosophical challenge here requires careful navigation between materialist reductionism and phenomenological respect for believer experience. Critics will immediately object that reducing religious belief to opportunistic adaptation ignores the genuine spiritual experiences that motivate authentic faith commitment. They argue correctly that many believers demonstrate remarkable consistency in their religious practices despite social costs, personal sacrifice, and material disadvantage. This critique demands acknowledgment that opportunistic belief adoption operates alongside other psychological mechanisms—including genuine mystical experience, moral conviction, and aesthetic attraction to religious symbols. However, recognizing these additional factors does not invalidate the opportunistic dimension. Even believers who experience genuine spiritual states must still navigate social contexts where religious expression carries practical consequences. The primate principle operates as one influence among many, shaping how individuals interpret and communicate their spiritual experiences within existing tribal frameworks.

Understanding mythic narrative construction requires distinguishing between factual accounts and symbolic narratives while avoiding the philosophical trap of treating this distinction as absolute. Anthropological analysis reveals that all human societies develop elaborate mythic traditions that serve multiple functions simultaneously: explaining natural phenomena, transmitting moral values, establishing social hierarchies, and providing emotional comfort in the face of uncertainty. These mythic narratives employ symbolic language that cannot be adequately understood through literal interpretation. Creation stories, flood legends, heroic journeys, and apocalyptic visions operate as what cognitive anthropologists term "analogical mental models"—symbolic frameworks that humans use to navigate complex social and environmental challenges by mapping familiar relationship patterns onto unfamiliar domains.

The symbolic analysis of religious narratives demands philosophical justification for treating these stories as human constructions rather than revealed truths. This methodology follows the interpretive anthropological tradition established by Clifford Geertz, who argued that cultures constitute "webs of significance" that humans themselves have spun, requiring interpretive rather than experimental analysis. Geertz's approach treats religious symbols as cultural texts that can be "read" to uncover their meaning-making functions within particular social contexts. However, this interpretive methodology must guard against the relativistic implication that all symbolic systems deserve equal epistemic respect. While acknowledging that religious symbols carry profound meaning for believers, anthropological analysis can simultaneously evaluate their truth claims against available evidence from history, archaeology, comparative mythology, and cognitive science.

Early ethnographic cases provide crucial evidence for understanding myth formation processes across diverse cultural contexts. Classical anthropological studies from Bronisław Malinowski, E.E. Evans-Pritchard, and Margaret Mead revealed remarkably consistent patterns in how traditional societies develop origin stories, ritual practices, and supernatural belief systems. These ethnographic accounts document how myths emerge to address universal human challenges: explaining natural phenomena before scientific methods developed, establishing social order in the absence of formal institutions, providing psychological comfort during crisis periods, and maintaining group cohesion across generational changes. Contemporary cognitive anthropology builds upon these ethnographic foundations by identifying the mental mechanisms that make mythic thinking universal across human societies.

However, ethnographic analysis of myth formation must confront the serious ethical and methodological challenges raised by postcolonial critics of anthropological authority. James Clifford's influential analysis reveals how traditional ethnographic writing constructed "ethnographic authority" through textual strategies that marginalized indigenous voices while privileging Western analytical frameworks. Earlier anthropologists often presented their interpretations of native beliefs as objective scientific knowledge while treating indigenous explanations as mere cultural data requiring external interpretation. This colonial dynamic produced ethnographic accounts that systematically misrepresented indigenous knowledge systems by filtering them through Western conceptual categories that indigenous peoples themselves might reject.

Contemporary anthropological practice attempts to address these concerns through methodological innovations that respect indigenous perspectives while maintaining analytical rigor. Rather than treating native informants as passive sources of data, current ethnographic methodology emphasizes collaborative research relationships that acknowledge indigenous peoples as intellectual partners with their own sophisticated theoretical frameworks. This approach recognizes that indigenous knowledge systems often contain insights about human psychology, ecological relationships, and social organization that complement and sometimes exceed Western academic knowledge. However, acknowledging indigenous intellectual contributions does not require abandoning critical analysis of religious claims. Ethnographic respect for indigenous perspectives can coexist with rigorous examination of how mythic narratives function as meaning-making systems rather than literal descriptions of supernatural realities.

The methodological challenge becomes particularly acute when analyzing indigenous creation myths, origin stories, and supernatural beliefs. Traditional anthropological approaches often treated these narratives as primitive attempts at scientific explanation that could be easily dismissed in favor of modern empirical knowledge. This approach reflected not only cultural arrogance but also fundamental misunderstanding of how mythic narratives function within indigenous societies. Contemporary anthropological practice recognizes that indigenous myths serve complex functions that extend far beyond primitive scientific explanation: they establish spiritual relationships with landscapes, encode environmental knowledge acquired over millennia, maintain social relationships across kinship networks, and provide frameworks for ethical decision-making that Western societies have not adequately replaced.

Respecting the sophisticated functions of indigenous mythic systems while maintaining critical analysis of their supernatural claims requires careful philosophical navigation. The analytical framework I propose treats indigenous myths with the same methodological approach applied to all religious traditions: acknowledging their cultural sophistication and social functions while subjecting their factual claims to evidential scrutiny. This approach recognizes that indigenous creation stories often contain remarkable ecological insights encoded in symbolic language, but it does not grant epistemic immunity to supernatural claims about divine creation, spiritual entities, or afterlife destinations. Indigenous knowledge systems deserve respect as intellectual achievements, but this respect does not require suspending critical evaluation of their metaphysical assumptions.

The emergence of myths to explain unknown phenomena reveals how human curiosity interacts with cognitive limitations to produce supernatural explanations. Before developing systematic methods of empirical investigation, our ancestors faced the same fundamental questions that drive contemporary scientific research: How did the universe begin? What causes natural disasters? Why do some individuals prosper while others suffer? How should social groups organize themselves? In the absence of controlled experimentation, mathematical modeling, and peer review processes, human intelligence inevitably generated explanatory frameworks based on available analogies drawn from familiar social experience. Creation myths typically employ metaphors derived from human reproduction, craftsmanship, or social organization because these represent the most complex causal processes that prescientific cultures could directly observe.

The anthropological record reveals remarkable consistency in mythic explanation patterns across geographically isolated societies, suggesting that universal cognitive mechanisms drive myth formation rather than cultural diffusion. Societies separated by oceans and millennia independently develop similar creation stories, flood narratives, hero journeys, and apocalyptic visions because human brains confronting similar explanatory challenges generate analogous symbolic solutions. This cognitive universality provides strong evidence against treating myths as culturally specific revelations and instead supports interpreting them as predictable products of human pattern-recognition systems applied to metaphysical questions beyond their original adaptive scope.

Religious myths also emerge to provide emotional comfort during periods of uncertainty, loss, and existential anxiety. Anthropological analysis reveals that mythic narratives consistently address universal human concerns about mortality, social conflict, natural disasters, and moral uncertainty. These stories provide psychological resources for managing anxiety by offering explanatory frameworks that render random suffering meaningful, establish cosmic justice systems that promise eventual moral vindication, and guarantee personal survival beyond biological death. The comfort-providing function of religious myths reflects genuine psychological needs that alternative worldviews must address if they hope to replace religious frameworks successfully.

However, acknowledging the comfort-providing function of religious myths does not validate their truth claims or justify their social consequences. Psychological comfort represents a legitimate human need, but false beliefs can provide temporary comfort while generating long-term harm through misdirected behavior, resource allocation, and social conflict. The critical analysis of religious myths must therefore distinguish between their psychological functions and their epistemic status, recognizing that narratives can serve important emotional needs while simultaneously propagating false information about natural phenomena, historical events, and moral relationships.

The transmission of cultural values through mythic narratives represents perhaps the most sophisticated function of religious storytelling systems. Religious myths encode complex moral intuitions, social expectations, and behavioral guidelines in memorable narrative forms that can be transmitted across generations through oral tradition and ritual practice. These stories serve as cultural technologies for maintaining social cooperation by establishing shared behavioral expectations, punishing free riders through supernatural sanctions, and rewarding cooperative behavior through divine approval. The value-transmission function of religious myths explains their remarkable persistence across cultural changes that might be expected to undermine supernatural belief systems.

Contemporary cognitive science reveals that narrative frameworks provide particularly effective mechanisms for moral education because story structures align with natural memory processes and emotional engagement systems. Humans remember moral principles more effectively when they are embedded in narrative contexts rather than presented as abstract rules, and they experience stronger emotional motivation to follow moral guidelines that are associated with compelling characters and dramatic consequences. Religious traditions that successfully encode moral wisdom in mythic narratives create more psychologically persuasive ethical systems than secular alternatives that rely primarily on rational argumentation or institutional enforcement.

Nevertheless, the effectiveness of religious narratives for transmitting cultural values does not exempt their moral content from critical evaluation. Many religious traditions encode moral intuitions that reflect the limited social experiences of their historical origins: tribal loyalty systems that justify violence against outsiders, patriarchal social arrangements that subordinate women's interests, hierarchical status systems that rationalize economic inequality, and anthropocentric environmental attitudes that ignore ecological relationships. The sophisticated narrative technologies that make religious moral transmission effective can serve regressive as well as progressive social functions. Critical analysis of religious myths must therefore evaluate both their transmission mechanisms and their substantive moral content.

The birth of myth reveals fundamental features of human psychology that extend far beyond religious contexts. Our species' capacity for storytelling, pattern recognition, and symbolic thinking provides the cognitive foundation for all cultural achievements: scientific theory construction, artistic expression, legal reasoning, and political organization all depend upon the same mental mechanisms that generate religious myths. However, recognizing the cognitive sophistication underlying mythic thinking does not validate supernatural belief systems or exempt religious claims from evidential scrutiny. Instead, understanding the psychological mechanisms that make myth-making inevitable provides crucial insights for developing more effective secular alternatives that can address genuine human needs currently served by religious frameworks while avoiding the epistemic and social costs that accompany supernatural belief systems.

The analysis presented here anticipates several predictable objections from religious apologists and postmodern critics. Religious defenders will argue that reducing religious beliefs to evolutionary byproducts ignores the transcendent dimensions of spiritual experience that cannot be captured through materialist analysis. Postmodern critics will contend that privileging scientific explanation over mythic narrative reflects Western cultural imperialism that marginalizes indigenous knowledge systems. Both critiques deserve serious consideration, but neither invalidates the analytical framework developed in this chapter. Acknowledging the evolutionary origins of religious cognition does not preclude recognizing the genuine value of spiritual experiences or the sophisticated cultural functions of mythic narratives. However, these acknowledgments do not require suspending critical evaluation of supernatural truth claims or granting epistemic immunity to religious belief systems. The goal of this analysis is not to eliminate the psychological and social functions currently served by religious myths, but rather to understand these functions sufficiently well to develop secular alternatives that can serve genuine human needs without perpetuating false beliefs about natural phenomena, historical events, and moral relationships.

Chapter Two
Defining Religion Across Cultures

The definitional problem in religious studies represents one of the most contentious and consequential challenges facing contemporary scholarship, revealing fundamental tensions between analytical necessity and postcolonial ethical responsibility. When anthropologists and religious studies scholars attempt to define religion as a universal category applicable across cultures, they immediately encounter what Talal Asad has identified as the definitional trap—the unavoidable reality that any universal definition of religion emerges from particular historical and cultural contexts, inevitably privileging certain forms of religious experience while marginalizing others. This challenge demands careful navigation between legitimate scholarly requirements for heuristic categories and the postcolonial critique that such definitions function as instruments of epistemic colonialism, imposing Western conceptual frameworks upon indigenous knowledge systems that organize spiritual experience according to fundamentally different principles.

The emergence of religion as a discrete analytical category reflects the specific historical trajectory of European Christianity and its encounter with secular modernity, rather than representing a natural or universal feature of human societies. Contemporary scholars increasingly recognize that the very concept of religion as "essentially a matter of symbolic meanings linked to ideas of general order" represents, in Asad's formulation, "a view that has a specific Christian history" rather than a culturally neutral descriptive framework. The modern Western understanding of religion as a private sphere of belief separated from public political life emerges from particular Protestant theological developments, Enlightenment rationality, and colonial administrative requirements rather than from universal human experience. This historical specificity poses serious challenges for cross-cultural analysis, as the application of Christian-derived definitional frameworks to non-Christian societies risks systematically misrepresenting indigenous spiritual traditions by filtering them through categories that those traditions themselves might reject.

The postcolonial critique of religious definitions, advanced most influentially by Talal Asad, reveals how supposedly universal analytical categories function as mechanisms of cultural hegemony and epistemic violence. Asad's genealogical approach demonstrates that the modern academic study of religion emerged during the height of European colonialism, when Western scholars developed theoretical frameworks designed to classify, compare, and ultimately control diverse spiritual traditions encountered in colonial territories. The definitional enterprise served colonial administrative purposes by creating manageable categories through which European authorities could understand and govern indigenous populations, often in ways that facilitated cultural transformation and political subordination. Contemporary postcolonial critics argue that continued reliance on Western-derived definitions perpetuates these colonial dynamics by maintaining intellectual frameworks that privilege European ways of organizing spiritual experience while marginalizing indigenous epistemologies.

However, the postcolonial critique of definitional universalism must be carefully distinguished from complete relativistic abandonment of cross-cultural analysis. While acknowledging the historical embeddedness of religious categories, scholars can defend the use of definitions as heuristic tools rather than imperial impositions by maintaining methodological transparency about their analytical frameworks and remaining open to revision based on ethnographic evidence. Definitions serve as provisional working hypotheses that enable comparative analysis across cultures while remaining subject to continuous refinement through encounter with diverse religious traditions. The key methodological requirement involves distinguishing between definitions as analytical conveniences and definitions as ontological claims about the essential nature of religious phenomena. When scholars approach religious definitions as flexible investigative tools rather than fixed conceptual boundaries, they can maintain analytical rigor while avoiding the epistemic colonialism that postcolonial critics rightfully identify as problematic.

The tribal lens represents another crucial dimension of the definitional challenge, as human cognitive architecture predisposes researchers toward interpretive frameworks that protect group identity and maintain social cohesion rather than pursuing objective analytical clarity. Religious studies scholars inevitably approach definitional questions through cultural lenses shaped by their own religious or secular backgrounds, creating systematic biases that favor familiar spiritual traditions while misunderstanding or marginalizing unfamiliar ones. These cognitive blind spots operate through confirmation bias mechanisms that lead researchers to interpret cross-cultural evidence in ways that support existing theoretical commitments while filtering out contradictory data. The tribal lens problem becomes particularly acute when Western-trained scholars study non-Western religious traditions, as their analytical frameworks may be fundamentally incompatible with indigenous ways of organizing spiritual experience.

Methodological safeguards against tribal lens distortion require systematic triangulation of sources, perspectives, and interpretive frameworks to identify and correct for systematic biases in definitional approaches. Effective triangulation involves consulting multiple types of evidence: ethnographic accounts from indigenous practitioners, historical documents from diverse cultural contexts, comparative analysis across geographically separated societies, and theoretical perspectives from scholars representing different cultural backgrounds. This methodological approach recognizes that no single perspective provides complete analytical access to religious phenomena, but that systematic comparison across multiple viewpoints can identify patterns that transcend particular cultural limitations. Contemporary religious studies increasingly emphasizes collaborative research methodologies that include indigenous scholars as intellectual partners rather than passive research subjects, ensuring that definitional frameworks remain accountable to diverse cultural perspectives.

The emic versus etic distinction provides essential analytical tools for navigating definitional challenges while maintaining respect for indigenous perspectives. Emic approaches prioritize insider understandings of religious experience, focusing on how practitioners themselves categorize, interpret, and explain their spiritual traditions rather than imposing external analytical frameworks. This methodology recognizes that religious participants possess sophisticated theoretical knowledge about their own traditions that may exceed outside scholarly understanding in important respects. Etic approaches employ comparative analytical frameworks designed to identify patterns across diverse religious traditions, enabling scholars to detect relationships and similarities that insider perspectives might not recognize. The challenge involves developing methodological frameworks that honor both emic and etic insights without subordinating either perspective to the other.

A robust methodological framework for balanced emic-etic analysis requires explicit acknowledgment of the complementary rather than competitive relationship between insider and outsider perspectives. Emic insights provide essential correctives to scholarly assumptions about religious phenomena, revealing how practitioners understand their own traditions and identifying analytical blind spots that external frameworks might generate. Etic insights enable comparative analysis that can identify universal patterns in religious experience while avoiding the particularistic limitations that might characterize individual traditions. Contemporary anthropological practice increasingly emphasizes dialogical methodologies that treat emic and etic perspectives as ongoing conversations rather than static positions, allowing for mutual correction and refinement of understanding through sustained intercultural engagement.

However, the methodological commitment to balanced emic-etic analysis does not require epistemic relativism that treats all insider claims as equally valid regardless of their relationship to available evidence. Scholars can maintain analytical rigor by distinguishing between phenomenological respect for insider experience and epistemic evaluation of truth claims about natural phenomena, historical events, and causal relationships. Religious practitioners may possess authoritative knowledge about the meaning and significance of their spiritual experiences while simultaneously holding beliefs about supernatural entities, miraculous events, or cosmological processes that contradict available scientific evidence. The methodological challenge involves honoring the sophisticated cultural knowledge that religious traditions contain while maintaining critical evaluation of factual claims that extend beyond immediate experiential domains.

The secular-religious binary represents perhaps the most problematic aspect of Western definitional frameworks, as this conceptual distinction reflects particular Protestant and Enlightenment assumptions rather than universal features of human societies. The notion that religion and politics, or spiritual and material concerns, constitute naturally separate domains emerges from specific historical circumstances rather than from cross-cultural analysis of how societies organize authority, meaning, and social relationships. Many indigenous traditions integrate spiritual, political, economic, and ecological concerns within unified worldview systems that resist decomposition into separate secular and religious spheres. Imposing secular-religious distinctions upon such traditions risks fundamentally misrepresenting their organizational logic and cultural significance.

Contemporary religious studies demonstrate increasing awareness of ongoing debates about the secular-religious binary and its analytical limitations. Post-secular theoretical approaches attempt to move beyond simple oppositional thinking that treats religion and secularity as mutually exclusive categories, instead exploring their complex historical co-constitution and ongoing interpenetration. These approaches recognize that secular institutions, ideologies, and practices often carry implicit religious assumptions, while religious traditions increasingly operate within and adapt to secular institutional contexts. The analytical goal involves developing conceptual frameworks that can account for the complex relationships between spiritual and material concerns without imposing rigid categorical boundaries that misrepresent lived cultural experience.

The challenges of cross-cultural definition become particularly evident when examining religious traditions that organize spiritual experience according to fundamentally different ontological and epistemological assumptions than those embedded in Western analytical frameworks. Indigenous knowledge systems often integrate spiritual, ecological, social, and technological dimensions within holistic frameworks that resist separation into discrete analytical domains. Traditional ecological knowledge, for example, combines empirical observation of natural phenomena with spiritual relationships to landscapes and ancestral wisdom transmission systems that Western academic categories struggle to accommodate. Defining such systems as "religious" in Western terms may capture certain aspects of their spiritual dimensions while missing crucial ecological, social, and technological components that indigenous practitioners consider inseparable from spiritual concerns.

Decolonizing approaches to religious definition emphasize the importance of respecting indigenous epistemologies and knowledge systems on their own terms rather than forcing them into Western analytical categories. This methodological commitment requires scholars to learn indigenous languages, engage with traditional knowledge holders as intellectual authorities, and develop analytical frameworks that can accommodate fundamentally different ways of organizing knowledge and experience. Decolonizing methodology does not require abandoning comparative analysis entirely, but it demands that such analysis proceed through respectful dialogue with indigenous intellectual traditions rather than through imposition of external categorical frameworks.

The definitional challenge reveals broader tensions between universalist aspirations of academic scholarship and particularist commitments of postcolonial ethics. Western academic institutions have historically claimed universal validity for their analytical methods and theoretical conclusions, treating European intellectual traditions as providing objective knowledge applicable across all cultural contexts. Postcolonial critics correctly identify this universalist pretension as a form of intellectual imperialism that marginalizes non-Western knowledge systems and perpetuates colonial power relationships. However, completely abandoning universalist analytical aspirations risks fragmenting academic discourse into incommensurable cultural perspectives that cannot engage in productive dialogue or collaborative knowledge production.

The methodological solution involves distinguishing between oppressive universalism that imposes particular cultural perspectives as universal truths and respectful universalism that seeks cross-cultural insights through dialogue among diverse intellectual traditions. Oppressive universalism treats Western analytical frameworks as providing privileged access to universal truths that other traditions must accept or risk being dismissed as prescientific or irrational. Respectful universalism recognizes that all intellectual traditions develop insights about universal human experiences, but that no single tradition possesses complete analytical access to these universals. This approach requires sustained intercultural dialogue that allows different knowledge traditions to inform and correct each other through ongoing collaborative inquiry.

The practical implications of definitional challenges extend beyond academic methodology to influence policy decisions, legal frameworks, and institutional practices that affect religious communities worldwide. Courts, governments, and international organizations regularly make decisions about religious freedom, minority rights, and cultural protection that depend upon definitions of religion derived from particular cultural traditions. When these definitions reflect Western Protestant assumptions about religion as private belief separated from public life, they may inadequately protect religious traditions that integrate spiritual and political dimensions or that organize community life according to different principles. The definitional challenge thus carries important practical consequences for religious communities seeking legal recognition, cultural protection, or institutional accommodation within secular legal frameworks.

Religious studies scholars face the ongoing challenge of developing definitional approaches that serve legitimate analytical purposes while respecting the cultural autonomy and epistemic authority of diverse religious traditions. This requires methodological innovations that can accommodate multiple perspectives simultaneously: insider understandings of particular traditions, comparative insights from cross-cultural analysis, and critical evaluation of truth claims about natural phenomena and historical events. Contemporary scholarship increasingly emphasizes collaborative methodologies that include indigenous scholars, religious practitioners, and community representatives as intellectual partners rather than passive research subjects, ensuring that definitional frameworks remain accountable to diverse cultural perspectives while maintaining analytical rigor.

The definitional challenge ultimately reveals the inherent tension between the analytical requirements of academic scholarship and the ethical demands of postcolonial responsibility. Scholars cannot abandon definitional frameworks entirely without rendering comparative analysis impossible, but they cannot impose Western-derived definitions without perpetuating colonial intellectual relationships. The solution requires ongoing methodological innovation that treats definitions as provisional, dialogical, and subject to continuous revision through encounter with diverse cultural perspectives. This approach maintains analytical rigor while respecting the intellectual autonomy of different religious traditions, creating space for genuine intercultural dialogue about the nature and significance of religious experience across human societies.

Critics will inevitably argue that this methodological approach remains insufficiently radical, as it continues to privilege academic analytical frameworks over indigenous knowledge systems, or alternatively, that it compromises scholarly objectivity by allowing cultural perspectives to influence analytical categories. Both critiques deserve serious consideration, but neither invalidates the approach developed here. The goal is not to eliminate all tensions between analytical and ethical requirements, but to develop methodological frameworks that can navigate these tensions responsibly while serving both scholarly and cultural needs. This requires ongoing commitment to methodological transparency, intercultural dialogue, and critical self-reflection about the cultural assumptions embedded in analytical frameworks. The definitional challenge in religious studies thus represents not a problem to be solved definitively, but an ongoing methodological responsibility that requires sustained attention and continuous refinement.

Chapter Three
Cognitive and Social Mechanisms

Human religious cognition emerges from the interaction of evolved cognitive biases, social reinforcement mechanisms, and neurological processes that collectively predispose our species toward supernatural belief systems. Understanding these mechanisms requires careful analysis of how agency detection systems, attentional limitations, ritual performance, opportunistic behavior, and brain chemistry contribute to religious experience while defending against the philosophical objections that such analysis inevitably provokes. The cognitive architecture underlying religious belief reflects millions of years of evolutionary adaptation to social environments where rapid threat detection, tribal solidarity, and resource competition determined survival, but these same mechanisms now generate elaborate supernatural explanations for phenomena that scientific investigation has rendered comprehensible through naturalistic means.

Agency detection represents perhaps the most fundamental cognitive mechanism underlying religious belief, operating through what researchers term the Hypersensitive Agency Detection Device (HADD)—a neural system that evolved to identify potential agents in ambiguous environmental stimuli. This system emerged from evolutionary pressures that made false positive errors (detecting agency where none exists) far less costly than false negative errors (missing actual agents that might pose threats or opportunities). Our ancestors who consistently detected predators, rivals, or allies in ambiguous sensory information survived at higher rates than those who failed to identify genuine agents, even if this hypervigilance occasionally generated phantom detections. Contemporary cognitive science demonstrates that this agency detection system remains hyperactive in modern humans, routinely attributing intentional causation to random events, natural phenomena, and complex systems that operate according to impersonal physical laws.

The replicability of cognitive science methods provides crucial defense against philosophical objections to agency detection research. Experimental studies consistently demonstrate that humans across diverse cultural backgrounds exhibit predictable patterns of agency attribution under controlled laboratory conditions. These findings emerge from rigorous experimental protocols that include double-blind procedures, statistical controls for confounding variables, and cross-cultural replication studies that ensure results reflect universal cognitive mechanisms rather than culturally specific interpretive frameworks. The Templeton Foundation's extensive research program on supernatural agency detection employs sophisticated physiological measurements, cognitive testing batteries, and neuroimaging techniques to identify the specific brain mechanisms underlying false positive agency attributions. Critics who dismiss agency detection research as reductionist materialism must confront the overwhelming experimental evidence demonstrating that religious cognition operates through identifiable, measurable, and replicable psychological processes.

However, recent theoretical developments challenge traditional modular accounts of agency detection by proposing predictive coding frameworks that better explain experimental findings. Marc Andersen's influential analysis argues that most false positives in agency detection result from Bayesian statistical processes in which the brain generates high prior probabilities for agent presence when confronting unreliable sensory stimuli. This predictive coding approach explains why agency detection varies dramatically across individuals and contexts—factors that simple modular theories struggle to accommodate. The brain's predictive machinery operates through sophisticated pattern recognition algorithms that constantly anticipate incoming sensory information, generating "prediction errors" when expectations fail to match reality. Religious experiences may represent systematic misfires of these prediction systems rather than outputs from dedicated supernatural detection modules.

Attentional tunnel-vision represents another crucial mechanism underlying religious cognition, reflecting evolutionary adaptations for focused threat detection that now constrain contemporary information processing in ways that favor religious interpretations. Our African savanna heritage equipped us with attentional systems designed to rapidly focus on potential dangers while filtering out irrelevant environmental details, a cognitive architecture that enhanced survival in environments where predator detection meant life or death. Contemporary humans inherit these same attentional biases, creating systematic blind spots that favor confirmatory evidence while screening out disconfirming information. Religious believers demonstrate particularly pronounced attentional tunnel-vision when confronting challenges to core beliefs, selectively attending to supportive evidence while dismissing contradictory data as irrelevant, misinterpreted, or motivated by hostile intentions.

The evolutionary advantages of attentional focus must be balanced against its contemporary costs for rational belief formation. Research demonstrates that confirmation bias can enhance group decision-making by encouraging division of cognitive labor, with different individuals pursuing different investigative strategies that collectively maximize information gathering. However, these same mechanisms become problematic when applied to metaphysical questions that require integrative analysis across multiple domains of evidence. Religious communities that successfully cultivate attentional tunnel-vision create more psychologically committed members but at the cost of epistemic accuracy and adaptability to changing circumstances.

Corrective reflective practices offer potential remedies for attentional limitations by training individuals to recognize and compensate for systematic cognitive biases. Contemporary cognitive science identifies several effective debiasing techniques: perspective-taking exercises that require considering alternative viewpoints, devil's advocate procedures that mandate engaging strongest counterarguments, and metacognitive training that develops awareness of one's own reasoning processes. Phenomenological reduction techniques, developed within the philosophical tradition established by Edmund Husserl, provide particularly sophisticated methods for suspending habitual assumptions and examining experience with reduced conceptual overlay. These practices require sustained effort and cannot eliminate cognitive biases entirely, but they can reduce their influence sufficiently to enable more accurate belief formation processes.

Victor Turner's ritual theory provides essential insights into the social mechanisms that reinforce religious beliefs through communal performance, but his analysis requires careful defense against charges of overgeneralization and transformationist bias. Turner's processual approach emphasizes how rituals function as social dramas that transition participants through liminal phases characterized by suspended normal social structures and heightened possibilities for identity transformation. During these liminal periods, participants experience what Turner terms communitas—intense feelings of social solidarity and shared identity that transcend ordinary hierarchical distinctions. Religious rituals exploit these liminal dynamics by creating controlled environments where supernatural narratives become psychologically compelling through emotional arousal, social pressure, and sensory manipulation.

Turner's concept of anti-structure reveals how religious rituals systematically invert normal social arrangements to generate transformative experiences that participants interpret as supernatural encounters. Ritual humiliation of authority figures, temporary suspension of social roles, and deliberate violation of ordinary behavioral norms create psychological states that religious traditions attribute to divine intervention rather than recognizing as predictable consequences of liminal social dynamics. The initiation of Ndembu kings through ritual humiliation exemplifies how religious traditions use anti-structural techniques to generate experiences that participants interpret as spiritual transformation while actually serving social control functions by reinforcing ultimate authority relationships.

However, Turner's ritual theory faces legitimate criticism for overemphasizing transformation while neglecting the conservative functions that many rituals serve. Ronald Grimes identifies "transformationism" as a problematic ideological assumption in Turner's work—the presumption that authentic rituals necessarily generate personal or social transformation rather than simply maintaining existing structures. Many religious rituals function primarily to reinforce established beliefs, strengthen group boundaries, and resist rather than promote change. Turner's focus on liminal anti-structure may reflect his own cultural bias toward progressive social transformation rather than accurate cross-cultural analysis of ritual functions.

Contemporary ritual studies address these concerns by developing more nuanced theoretical frameworks that acknowledge both transformative and conservative ritual functions without privileging either dimension a priori. This approach recognizes that rituals serve multiple functions simultaneously: some aspects may promote transformation while others maintain stability, and the same ritual may function differently for different participants or in different historical contexts. The theoretical challenge involves developing analytical frameworks that can account for this functional complexity without losing explanatory power or predictive capacity.

The opportunistic and amoral dimensions of human nature profoundly shape religious belief adoption and expression, reflecting evolutionary inheritance from primate ancestors who survived through strategic behavioral flexibility rather than consistent moral principles. Evolutionary psychology demonstrates that humans routinely calibrate their behavioral strategies based on environmental feedback about costs and benefits, including the social advantages that accompany religious participation within particular cultural contexts. Religious beliefs often function as strategic signals that communicate group membership, moral reliability, and cooperative intentions to potential allies, partners, and authorities who control access to valuable resources. Understanding this opportunistic dimension requires careful distinction between descriptive evolutionary accounts and normative moral evaluations of contemporary religious behavior.

Opportunistic religious adoption operates through life-history strategic decisions that reflect unconscious calculations about optimal resource allocation across different environmental contexts. Individuals facing harsh, unpredictable, or competitive environments tend toward "fast" life-history strategies characterized by immediate gratification, risk-taking, and flexible social commitments, while those in stable, secure, predictable environments tend toward "slow" strategies emphasizing long-term planning, delayed gratification, and sustained social investments. Religious beliefs and practices often serve as adaptive responses to these environmental pressures: conversion experiences frequently follow personal crises, religious intensity correlates with socioeconomic stress, and denominational switching reflects strategic responses to changing social circumstances rather than theological conviction.

The distinction between explanation and justification becomes crucial when analyzing opportunistic religious behavior. Evolutionary explanations for religious opportunism describe psychological mechanisms that influence belief adoption without morally endorsing or condemning these behaviors. When cognitive science demonstrates that humans unconsciously adjust religious commitments based on social advantages, this descriptive account does not imply that such behavior is morally appropriate or that religious beliefs lack genuine spiritual significance for practitioners. Many individuals experience authentic spiritual states while simultaneously receiving social benefits from religious participation, and these dual motivations may reinforce rather than undermine each other.

Critics will object that characterizing religious behavior as opportunistic reduces genuine spiritual experience to mere social calculation, ignoring the profound personal meaning that religious traditions provide for billions of believers. This objection deserves serious consideration but conflates explanatory levels that can and should remain distinct. Evolutionary analysis of opportunistic tendencies operates at the level of unconscious psychological mechanisms that influence behavior across all domains, not just religion. These mechanisms shape how individuals interpret and respond to spiritual experiences without determining the content or significance of those experiences. Understanding the opportunistic dimensions of religious behavior enhances rather than diminishes appreciation for the complex psychological processes underlying spiritual life.

The neuroscience of religious experience provides increasingly sophisticated accounts of the brain mechanisms underlying spiritual states, but these findings must be interpreted carefully to avoid reductionist oversimplification while acknowledging genuine phenomenological insights. Neuroimaging studies consistently identify specific brain regions that activate during prayer, meditation, and other religious practices: the prefrontal cortex (associated with focused attention), temporal lobes (linked to religious imagery and emotions), and limbic system (involved in emotional processing and reward mechanisms). These neurological patterns appear remarkably consistent across different religious traditions, suggesting that spiritual experiences reflect universal brain processes rather than culturally specific interpretive frameworks.

Andrew Newberg's pioneering SPECT and fMRI studies demonstrate that religious practices produce measurable changes in brain activity and structure, particularly in regions associated with attention, memory, and emotional regulation. Participants who engage in regular meditation or prayer show enhanced cognitive performance, improved emotional stability, and increased activity in brain areas linked to positive affect and social bonding. These findings provide objective evidence that religious practices generate genuine psychological benefits through identifiable neurological mechanisms, lending scientific credibility to subjective reports of spiritual transformation and well-being.

However, neurotheological research faces legitimate criticism for conflating correlation with causation and for making excessive claims about the relationship between brain activity and spiritual reality. The fact that religious experiences produce distinctive brain activation patterns does not necessarily mean that spirituality reduces to neurological processes, any more than the brain activity associated with music appreciation proves that musical beauty exists only in neural firing patterns. Neuroscience describes the biological substrate of conscious experience without explaining the subjective meaning or potential transcendent significance of that experience.

The limits of reductionism become particularly evident when neuroscientific findings are integrated with phenomenological analyses of religious experience. Phenomenology examines the structure and content of conscious experience from the first-person perspective, focusing on how phenomena appear to consciousness rather than their underlying causal mechanisms. Religious experiences often possess distinctive phenomenological features—sense of presence, feelings of transcendence, perception of ultimate meaning—that resist reduction to neurological descriptions even when their brain correlates are well understood. The challenge involves developing theoretical frameworks that can acknowledge both the neurological substrate and phenomenological content of religious experience without reducing either dimension to the other.

Contemporary philosophy of mind increasingly recognizes that consciousness poses fundamental explanatory challenges that purely reductionist approaches cannot resolve. The "hard problem of consciousness"—explaining how subjective experience emerges from objective physical processes—remains unsolved despite remarkable advances in neuroscientific understanding of brain mechanisms. Religious experiences may provide particularly clear examples of this explanatory gap, as they often involve qualitative states of consciousness that seem to transcend their neurological substrates. Acknowledging this explanatory limitation does not require abandoning scientific investigation of religious experience, but it does counsel methodological humility about the scope and implications of neuroscientific findings.

The distinction between methodological atheism and ontological materialism provides essential conceptual clarity for navigating the relationship between scientific investigation and religious truth claims. Methodological atheism brackets questions about the existence or non-existence of supernatural entities to enable empirical investigation of religious phenomena, while ontological materialism makes substantive metaphysical claims about the ultimate nature of reality. Contemporary anthropology and religious studies increasingly recognize that methodological atheism represents the appropriate stance for scholarly investigation, as it enables rigorous analysis of religious beliefs and practices without requiring researchers to adopt particular metaphysical commitments.

Peter Berger's influential formulation of methodological atheism requires that religious beliefs be subjected to sociological scrutiny "on the assumption that they are not literally true" while remaining agnostic about their ultimate truth status. This methodological stance enables scholars to analyze the social and psychological functions of religious beliefs without dismissing their potential spiritual significance or making claims beyond the scope of empirical investigation. The approach recognizes that scientific methods cannot definitively resolve questions about supernatural reality while maintaining that they can illuminate the human dimensions of religious experience.

However, methodological atheism faces criticism from both religious believers and secular materialists for different reasons. Religious critics argue that bracketing truth claims inevitably marginalizes religious perspectives and reduces spiritual experiences to mere psychological phenomena, while secular critics contend that maintaining agnosticism about supernatural claims provides unwarranted intellectual respectability to irrational beliefs. Both critiques misunderstand the methodological purpose of bracketing, which aims to enable rigorous empirical investigation rather than make substantive claims about religious truth or falsity.

The ontological turn in anthropology challenges methodological atheism by arguing that scholars should take indigenous beliefs seriously as potential descriptions of reality rather than treating them as cultural constructions requiring explanation. This approach suggests that supernatural agents, spiritual forces, and non-material realities described by religious practitioners might exist in ways that conventional scientific frameworks cannot accommodate. While this perspective deserves serious consideration as a corrective to reductionist tendencies, it risks abandoning the epistemological standards that enable scholarly knowledge to transcend particular cultural perspectives.

The resolution involves maintaining commitment to bracketed analysis while acknowledging the phenomenological validity of religious experience and the potential limitations of current scientific paradigms. This approach treats religious truth claims as worthy of respectful consideration while subjecting them to the same evidential standards applied to other empirical assertions. The goal is not to debunk or validate religious beliefs but to understand their psychological, social, and cultural functions through rigorous analytical methods that remain accountable to available evidence.

The integration of cognitive, social, and neurological mechanisms reveals religious belief as emerging from the complex interaction of evolved psychological dispositions, cultural transmission processes, and individual developmental experiences. Agency detection biases predispose humans toward supernatural explanations, attentional limitations create systematic blind spots that favor confirmatory evidence, ritual practices generate powerful psychological states through social manipulation, opportunistic tendencies encourage strategic religious adoption, and neurological processes provide the biological substrate for spiritual experiences. These mechanisms operate simultaneously and interactively, creating feedback loops that reinforce religious beliefs while making them resistant to disconfirming evidence.

Understanding these mechanisms provides crucial insights for developing secular alternatives that can address genuine human needs currently served by religious frameworks without perpetuating false beliefs about natural phenomena, historical events, or moral relationships. Effective secular worldviews must acknowledge and accommodate the psychological functions that make religious beliefs compelling: meaning-making narratives, social solidarity, emotional regulation, moral guidance, and transcendent experiences. The challenge involves creating cultural institutions and practices that serve these functions through naturalistic means while maintaining intellectual honesty about the current limits of human knowledge and understanding.

Critics will inevitably argue that this analysis reduces the richness and complexity of religious experience to mechanistic psychological processes, ignoring the genuine spiritual insights and moral wisdom that religious traditions provide. This criticism deserves acknowledgment while maintaining that understanding the psychological mechanisms underlying religious experience does not diminish its personal significance or cultural value. The goal is not to eliminate religious experience but to understand it sufficiently well to distinguish its beneficial aspects from its problematic consequences, enabling more informed decisions about which elements of traditional religious life deserve preservation and which require transformation or replacement in contemporary contexts.

Chapter Four
Creation Myths and Cosmologies

Creation myths represent humanity's earliest and most fundamental attempts to explain the ultimate questions that emerge from conscious awareness: Why does anything exist rather than nothing? How did the complex order we observe emerge from apparent chaos? What is our place and purpose within the vast cosmos we inhabit? These questions transcend cultural boundaries and historical epochs, generating remarkably consistent mythological responses across geographically isolated societies that developed independently over millennia. From the Aboriginal Dreamtime stories of Australia to the Babylonian Enuma Elish, from Hindu cosmological cycles to indigenous American earth-emergence narratives, human cultures have constructed elaborate symbolic frameworks to address existential mysteries that scientific investigation has only recently begun to illuminate through empirical methods. The comparative analysis of creation myths reveals both the universal psychological needs that drive mythological thinking and the cultural specificity that shapes how different societies express these fundamental human concerns.

The cross-cultural analysis of origin stories demands respectful engagement with indigenous knowledge systems while maintaining analytical rigor about their factual accuracy and explanatory adequacy. Creation myths serve multiple sophisticated functions simultaneously: they provide psychological comfort in the face of existential uncertainty, establish social hierarchies and moral frameworks, encode ecological knowledge about local environments, and create shared identity markers that distinguish in-groups from out-groups. The Aboriginal Dreamtime traditions of Australia, for example, integrate creation narratives with detailed environmental knowledge, social law, ceremonial practice, and spiritual beliefs within unified cosmological systems that have sustained complex societies for over 65,000 years. These traditions cannot be adequately understood through simple categorization as "primitive science" or dismissed as mere fantasy, but require sophisticated analytical frameworks that can acknowledge their cultural complexity while evaluating their empirical claims about natural phenomena and historical events.

The respect for narrative value alongside critical analysis becomes particularly crucial when examining how creation myths function as meaning-making systems within their original cultural contexts. The Vedic creation hymns of ancient India, including the famous Nasadiya Sukta (Hymn of Creation), demonstrate remarkable philosophical sophistication in their treatment of ultimate questions about existence and causation. The Rigveda 10.129 passage explicitly acknowledges the limitations of human knowledge about ultimate origins: "Who verily knows and who can here declare it, whence it was born and whence comes this creation? The gods are later than this world's production. Who knows then whence it first came into being?". This epistemological humility contrasts sharply with the confident assertions about divine creation found in many religious traditions, suggesting that some ancient cultures developed nuanced philosophical frameworks for approaching cosmological questions that anticipate contemporary scientific methodology in important respects.

However, acknowledging the philosophical sophistication of creation myths does not require accepting their supernatural claims or treating them as equivalent to scientific explanations. The Hindu cosmological concept of cyclical time, with its elaborate calculations of cosmic ages (yugas) extending over billions of years, demonstrates impressive mathematical imagination while simultaneously incorporating supernatural elements—divine avatars, cosmic serpents, primordial deities—that lack empirical support. The analytical challenge involves distinguishing between the genuine insights that traditional cosmologies may contain about time, causation, and cosmic scale from their empirically unsupported assertions about supernatural agents and miraculous events. Contemporary astrophysics has validated some aspects of Hindu temporal concepts while definitively rejecting others, requiring careful discrimination between different types of claims embedded within unified mythological systems.

The Mesopotamian Enuma Elish provides a particularly instructive case study for understanding how creation myths function as political instruments while simultaneously addressing genuine cosmological questions. This elaborate seven-tablet epic, composed around 1200 BCE but drawing on much earlier Sumerian traditions, describes the emergence of order from primordial chaos through violent conflict between cosmic forces personified as deities. The narrative progression from initial void (represented by the freshwater Apsu and saltwater Tiamat) through generational conflict among divine beings to final cosmic ordering under Marduk's sovereignty parallels patterns found in creation stories worldwide, suggesting either common psychological origins or cultural diffusion across ancient Near Eastern societies. The political function becomes explicit in the text's conclusion, where Marduk creates humanity specifically to serve the gods and establishes Babylon as the cosmic center, clearly legitimizing both religious hierarchies and political authority structures.

The comparative analysis reveals recurring thematic patterns that appear across geographically isolated cultures, suggesting either common cognitive origins or ancient cultural connections that predate recorded history. The motif of creation from cosmic eggs appears in traditions as diverse as Finnish Kalevala, Chinese cosmology, Hindu Hiranyagarbha myths, and various African creation stories. The pattern of generational conflict among primordial beings—with older chaotic forces being overthrown by younger divine generations who establish cosmic order—occurs in Greek Titanomachy, Germanic Ragnarok, Hindu conflicts between devas and asuras, and numerous other traditions. The earth-emergence theme, in which dry land rises from primordial waters through divine intervention, appears in biblical flood narratives, Mesopotamian creation accounts, indigenous American stories, and many other cultural contexts.

These cross-cultural patterns demand explanation, and several competing hypotheses have emerged from comparative mythology and cognitive anthropology. The psychological hypothesis, influenced by Carl Jung's archetypal theory, suggests that creation myths reflect universal patterns inherent in human cognitive architecture—evolved mental templates that predispose all cultures toward similar symbolic expressions of fundamental existential concerns. The diffusionist hypothesis argues that thematic similarities reflect ancient cultural transmission through trade networks, migration patterns, and conquest dynamics that spread mythological motifs across vast geographical distances over extended time periods. The environmental hypothesis proposes that similar ecological challenges—flood cycles, seasonal changes, astronomical observations—generate comparable mythological responses across different societies facing analogous natural phenomena.

The most plausible explanation likely combines elements from all three hypotheses while avoiding reductive oversimplification. Human cognitive architecture undoubtedly creates predispositions toward certain types of explanatory frameworks: agency detection systems encourage supernatural explanations, pattern recognition mechanisms generate symbolic thinking, and social cognition promotes anthropomorphic projections onto natural phenomena. However, these universal cognitive tendencies interact with particular environmental circumstances and historical cultural exchanges to produce the specific mythological traditions we observe. The remarkable similarities between Mesopotamian and biblical creation accounts, for example, clearly reflect documented cultural contact during the Babylonian exile rather than independent psychological convergence.

The Aboriginal Australian creation traditions provide particularly valuable insights into how mythology functions as integrated knowledge systems that resist easy categorization into separate domains. Dreamtime stories describe the journeys of ancestral spirits across the landscape during creation epochs, but these narratives simultaneously encode practical information about water sources, seasonal patterns, plant and animal behavior, kinship obligations, ceremonial procedures, and social law. The Rainbow Serpent traditions found across much of northern Australia describe cosmic creation through the movements of giant serpentine beings, but these stories also contain sophisticated ecological knowledge about river systems, weather patterns, and landscape formation. The songlines or "dreaming tracks" that cross the continent function as both mythological narratives and practical navigation systems that enable travel across vast distances through complex terrain.

The cultural sophistication of Aboriginal traditions becomes particularly evident when compared to the mechanistic reductionism that characterized early anthropological interpretations. Colonial administrators and missionaries typically dismissed Dreamtime stories as primitive superstitions that reflected prescientific thinking about natural phenomena, failing to recognize their function as complex epistemological systems that integrate empirical observation, social organization, spiritual practice, and philosophical reflection within unified cultural frameworks. Contemporary anthropological analysis reveals that these traditions contain sophisticated insights about landscape formation, species relationships, astronomical phenomena, and human psychology that complement rather than contradict scientific understanding in many important respects.

However, respecting the cultural sophistication of indigenous knowledge systems does not require abandoning critical evaluation of their factual claims about supernatural entities, miraculous events, or cosmological processes. The analytical framework developed here maintains that mythological traditions deserve respectful engagement as intellectual achievements while simultaneously subjecting their empirical assertions to evidential scrutiny. Aboriginal creation stories about the Rainbow Serpent carving river systems and mountain ranges encode genuine geographical knowledge while simultaneously making claims about supernatural agency that lack empirical support. The challenge involves developing analytical methods that can separate valuable ecological and social insights

RELIGION AS A MIND PAINTING

from empirically unsupported supernatural assertions without dismissing entire knowledge systems as primitive or irrational.

The Hindu cosmological traditions present particularly complex interpretive challenges because of their remarkable integration of mathematical precision, philosophical sophistication, and supernatural mythology. The Puranic literature describes cosmic cycles spanning billions of years, with detailed calculations of temporal relationships between different scales of existence that anticipate modern astronomical discoveries about cosmic time. The concept of multiple universes existing simultaneously, each following its own temporal trajectory through cycles of creation and destruction, bears striking resemblances to contemporary cosmological theories about multiverse scenarios and cyclical cosmologies. The Vedic description of cosmic expansion from primordial unity into manifest diversity parallels Big Bang cosmology in suggestive ways, while the treatment of time as fundamental cosmic principle anticipates relativity theory's integration of space and time.

Nevertheless, these remarkable anticipations occur within mythological frameworks that simultaneously assert supernatural claims about divine avatars, cosmic serpents, primordial deities, and miraculous interventions that contradict available scientific evidence. The Vishnu Purana describes creation as emerging from Vishnu's cosmic dream, with Brahma arising from a lotus growing from Vishnu's navel to perform the work of material manifestation. While this imagery may function effectively as metaphorical description of consciousness and material reality relationships, treating it as literal cosmological account requires accepting supernatural agents and processes that lack empirical support. The analytical task involves carefully distinguishing between mythological insights that may contain genuine wisdom about time, consciousness, and cosmic relationships from empirically unsupported assertions about supernatural entities and miraculous events.

The comparison between mythic narratives and scientific cosmology requires careful articulation of different epistemic domains while avoiding both relativistic conflation and scientistic dismissal. Scientific cosmology operates through empirical observation, mathematical modeling, experimental testing, and peer review processes that generate increasingly accurate descriptions of natural phenomena and their causal relationships. The Big Bang theory emerges from multiple converging lines of evidence: cosmic microwave background radiation, galactic redshift patterns, light element abundances, and large-scale structure formation that collectively support the conclusion that our observable universe expanded from an extremely hot, dense initial state approximately 13.8 billion years ago. These conclusions rest on reproducible observations, mathematical consistency, predictive success, and international scientific consensus rather than cultural tradition, religious authority, or subjective experience.

Mythic cosmologies, by contrast, operate through symbolic narrative, cultural transmission, religious authority, and interpretive tradition to generate meaning-making frameworks that address existential questions about purpose, value, and cosmic significance that scientific method cannot directly investigate. The Babylonian Enuma Elish addresses questions about cosmic purpose, divine justice, human destiny, and social order that remain relevant to contemporary existence despite the text's scientifically obsolete assertions about physical cosmology. The Aboriginal Dreamtime traditions provide frameworks for understanding human relationships to landscape, ancestors, and cosmic forces that serve important psychological and social functions despite their empirically unsupported claims about supernatural creation events.

The recognition of different epistemic domains does not require treating scientific and mythological approaches as equally valid ways of understanding natural phenomena. Scientific methodology has demonstrated remarkable success in generating accurate predictions about natural phenomena, technological applications that transform human life, and cross-cultural consensus about empirical relationships that transcend particular cultural perspectives. Creation myths, while serving important psychological and social functions, consistently make empirically false claims about natural phenomena, historical events, and causal relationships that scientific investigation has definitively contradicted. The age of the earth, the evolutionary origins of species, the formation of geological features, and the development of human societies all differ dramatically from mythological accounts when subjected to empirical investigation.

However, acknowledging the empirical superiority of scientific explanation does not eliminate the analytical challenge posed by creation myths' persistent psychological and cultural appeal. Billions of contemporary people continue finding mythological accounts more personally meaningful than scientific explanations, despite widespread access to scientific education and overwhelming empirical evidence for naturalistic cosmology. This persistent preference for mythological over scientific explanation requires serious analytical attention rather than dismissive ridicule. Creation myths address existential questions about ultimate purpose, cosmic meaning, and human destiny that scientific methodology cannot directly investigate, while providing narrative frameworks that integrate cognitive, emotional, and social dimensions of human experience in ways that technical scientific discourse typically cannot match.

The theological versus anthropological interpretation of creation myths represents a crucial methodological distinction that determines how scholars approach these materials and what types of conclusions they draw from comparative analysis. Theological approaches treat creation myths as potential sources of revealed truth about ultimate reality, divine nature, and cosmic purpose, typically privileging particular traditions while defending their supernatural claims against scientific criticism. Anthropological approaches treat creation myths as cultural artifacts that reveal important information about human psychology, social organization, and meaning-making processes without requiring acceptance of their supernatural assertions. The choice between theological and anthropological interpretive frameworks fundamentally shapes both methodology and conclusions in ways that require explicit acknowledgment and defense.

The anthropological approach adopted here treats creation myths as sophisticated cultural achievements that deserve respectful analysis while maintaining methodological commitment to empirical evaluation of their factual claims. This approach avoids the strawman caricatures that often characterize debates between religious and secular interpreters by acknowledging the genuine insights that mythological traditions may contain about human experience, psychological needs, and social organization while simultaneously maintaining critical evaluation of their empirical assertions about natural phenomena and historical events. The goal involves understanding why creation myths persist across cultures and continue appealing to contemporary audiences rather than simply debunking their supernatural elements or defending their religious authority.

The anthropological framework enables recognition that creation myths serve multiple legitimate functions that scientific cosmology cannot directly address: providing narrative coherence to human experience, establishing moral frameworks for social behavior, creating emotional connections to cosmic processes, and generating meaning-making resources for confronting existential challenges like mortality, suffering, and uncertainty. The Mesopotamian Enuma Elish addresses questions about cosmic justice, divine authority, and human purpose that remain psychologically compelling despite the text's scientifically obsolete cosmological assertions. The Hindu cyclical cosmologies provide frameworks for understanding temporal relationships, consciousness, and ultimate reality that offer resources for philosophical reflection despite their supernatural mythology. The Aboriginal Dreamtime traditions create integrated knowledge systems that connect ecological awareness, social responsibility, and spiritual practice in ways that mechanistic scientific approaches struggle to match.

Nevertheless, acknowledging the legitimate cultural functions of creation myths does not require treating their empirical claims as immune from critical evaluation or epistemically equivalent to scientific explanation. The anthropological approach maintains that mythological traditions can serve important human needs while simultaneously making false assertions about natural phenomena that deserve correction through scientific investigation. Understanding why humans create and maintain creation myths enhances rather than undermines critical evaluation of their truth claims, as it reveals the psychological and social mechanisms that make supernatural explanations appealing independent of their empirical accuracy.

The cross-cultural evidence reveals that creation myths consistently exhibit certain structural features that reflect universal cognitive and social mechanisms rather than accurate observation of cosmic processes. The anthropomorphic projection of human social relationships onto cosmic processes appears in virtually all creation traditions: deities that reproduce, compete, negotiate, and establish hierarchical relationships mirror the social dynamics familiar to their human creators rather than representing genuinely cosmic principles. The emphasis on intentional creation by conscious agents reflects evolved agency detection systems that predispose humans toward supernatural explanation rather than empirically supported conclusions about natural causation. The focus on creation events in the distant past that establish permanent cosmic order serves psychological needs for meaning and stability rather than accurately describing ongoing natural processes that scientific cosmology reveals.

These universal patterns suggest that creation myths reveal more about human psychology than cosmic history, providing valuable data for understanding evolved cognitive mechanisms, social organization principles, and meaning-making strategies rather than reliable information about the actual origins and structure of the physical universe. This conclusion does not diminish the cultural value or personal significance of creation myths, but it does clarify their proper epistemic status as human constructions rather than revealed cosmic truths. The persistent appeal of mythological over scientific explanation reflects the match between mythological narratives and evolved psychological needs rather than the superior empirical accuracy of supernatural accounts.

The implications of this analysis extend beyond academic debates about mythology and science to contemporary challenges about education, public policy, and cultural conflict. Societies that maintain creation myths as literal descriptions of cosmic history face ongoing tensions with scientific education, environmental policy, and international dialogue that requires resolution through careful discrimination between different types of truth claims and their appropriate domains of application. The solution involves neither abandoning scientific methodology in favor of mythological authority nor dismissing mythological traditions as worthless superstitions, but rather developing sophisticated cultural frameworks that can honor the genuine insights and legitimate functions of creation myths while maintaining commitment to empirical accuracy about natural phenomena and historical events. This requires both intellectual sophistication and cultural sensitivity that contemporary educational institutions and public discourse often lack, creating ongoing challenges for navigating the relationship between traditional wisdom and scientific knowledge in pluralistic societies.

Chapter Five
Miracles, Revelation, and Authority

Religion has always claimed to speak with a voice unlike any other. Political rulers may command armies, scientists may marshal evidence, but prophets and priests have claimed to speak with the authority of the divine. Their words are not merely persuasive; they are binding. Their stories are not merely inspiring; they are miraculous. Their institutions are not merely powerful; they are sacred. For centuries, these claims were accepted as self evident. To question them was to risk not only social ostracism but eternal damnation. Yet the modern world has subjected these claims to relentless scrutiny. Historians have dissected sacred texts with the same tools they apply to any ancient manuscript. Psychologists have probed visions and revelations, seeking their roots in the human mind. Philosophers have asked whether the very idea of a miracle or a revelation is coherent. And yet, despite this sustained assault, religion persists. It continues to inspire devotion, to shape cultures, to command loyalty. The persistence of religion in the face of critique demands explanation. Why do miracles, revelation, and authority still matter, even when their epistemic foundations have been so thoroughly undermined?

The historian's critique began in earnest during the Renaissance and Enlightenment. Lorenzo Valla's exposure of the Donation of Constantine as a forgery was a harbinger of things to come: documents once treated as sacred could be unmasked as human inventions. Spinoza's insistence that the Bible must be read like any other book shattered the assumption that scripture was immune to reason. By the eighteenth and nineteenth centuries, biblical criticism had become a sophisticated discipline. Scholars developed tools such as source criticism, which sought to identify the earlier documents behind the Pentateuch; form criticism, which traced the oral traditions that shaped the Gospels; and redaction criticism, which examined how editors shaped theological emphases. The result was a picture of scripture not as a seamless divine revelation but as a patchwork of human voices, stitched together over centuries. The miracle stories that once seemed to testify to divine intervention now appeared as literary tropes, echoing motifs from Greco Roman biography and Jewish apocalyptic literature. The feeding of the five thousand, for example, could be read not as a supernatural multiplication of loaves but as a symbolic enactment of divine abundance, recalling the manna in the wilderness. The resurrection narratives, far from being straightforward historical reportage, bore the marks of theological reflection and communal memory.

David Hume sharpened the critique with philosophical precision. In his famous essay "Of Miracles," he argued that no testimony could ever suffice to establish a violation of natural law. Our experience of the uniformity of nature is so strong that any report of a miracle is always more likely to be false than true. Even multiple witnesses cannot overcome this imbalance, for it is always more probable that they are deceived or mistaken than that the laws of nature have been suspended. Hume's argument did not merely cast doubt on particular miracle claims; it undermined the very possibility of miracles serving as evidence for religion. If miracles cannot be believed on testimony, then they cannot function as the foundation of faith.

The historical critical method and Hume's skepticism together destabilized the epistemic role of miracles. They could no longer serve as proofs of divine authority. At best, they could be understood as symbolic narratives, theological constructions, or communal memories. Yet defenders of miracles have not been silent. Richard Swinburne has argued that miracles can be assessed probabilistically. If the existence of God is already judged to be more probable than not, then reports of miracles can, under certain conditions, be rationally accepted. Alvin Plantinga has gone further, insisting that belief in God and in divine action can be "properly basic," rational without requiring evidential proof. Karl Barth, in a different register, insisted that revelation is not a human construction but a divine act that breaks into history. Rudolf Bultmann sought to preserve the meaning of miracle stories by "demythologizing" them, stripping away their supernatural clothing to reveal existential truths. These defenses show that the debate is not one sided. Yet they also reveal the limits of defense. Swinburne's probabilistic calculus depends on prior theistic commitments; Plantinga's "properly basic" belief secures rationality for the believer but not persuasion for the skeptic; Barth's insistence on revelation as sui generis removes it from the realm of critique but also from the realm of verification. The defenses preserve faith, but they do not restore epistemic certainty. They show that miracles can still be meaningful, but not that they can function as universally compelling evidence.

If the historian dissects texts, the psychologist listens to experiences. Psychology has long sought to naturalize revelation. Ludwig Feuerbach argued that God is nothing more than the projection of human ideals. In The Essence of Christianity, he claimed that the attributes ascribed to God—love, wisdom, justice—are in fact the highest qualities of humanity, alienated from the self and projected onto a divine screen. Religion, in this view, is humanity worshipping its own essence without realizing it. Freud radicalized this critique by interpreting religion as illusion. In The Future of an Illusion, he argued that religious beliefs are wish fulfillments, born of humanity's helplessness in the face of nature and mortality. Miracles are fantasies of protection, revelation is the voice of the father internalized, and authority is the continuation of parental control into adulthood. Religion, for Freud, is a collective neurosis, a necessary stage in cultural development but one that must eventually be overcome. The psychological critique here is not merely descriptive but normative: religion is not only explicable but pathological. Its persistence is a sign of immaturity, its decline a mark of progress.

Yet psychology has also provided defenses. William James, in his Varieties of Religious Experience, conceded the natural basis of mystical states but argued that their pragmatic fruits—greater courage, moral transformation, existential peace—are what confer legitimacy. A vision that produces compassion cannot be dismissed simply because it has neural correlates. Paul Tillich reframed revelation as the disclosure of "ultimate concern," not as supernatural interruption but as the unveiling of what matters most. Modern neuroscience has confirmed that mystical states often lead to greater resilience, altruism, and well being. Even if they are "mind paintings," they are paintings that change lives. The reductionist dilemma is clear: to explain the mechanism of an experience is not to adjudicate its meaning. Revelation cannot be verified externally. Its authority is always mediated through subjective conviction and communal validation. Yet this very subjectivity is what makes revelation powerful. It cannot be disproven by external critique because it does not rest on external verification. The psychological critique thus destabilizes revelation as an epistemic category while leaving intact its existential and pragmatic force. Revelation may not disclose objective truths about the cosmos, but it discloses truths about the human condition—truths that shape lives, inspire communities, and sustain hope.

Religion is not only a matter of texts and experiences; it is also a matter of communities, institutions, and the structures of authority that bind them together. If the historian destabilizes miracles and the psychologist reduces revelation to projection, the sociologist asks how authority is generated, maintained, and contested. Max Weber's typology of authority remains foundational here. He distinguished between charismatic authority, traditional authority, and rational legal authority. Charismatic authority arises from the extraordinary personality of a leader, someone who seems to embody divine power or unique insight. Traditional authority rests on the sanctity of inherited customs and institutions. Rational legal authority depends on codified rules and bureaucratic structures. Religion, Weber argued, often begins with charisma: the prophet who speaks with the voice of God, the mystic who radiates holiness, the healer who performs wonders. But charisma is unstable. It must be routinized if it is to endure. The prophet dies, and his followers must decide how to preserve his message. The mystic's visions must be written down, the healer's practices institutionalized. Charisma becomes tradition, and tradition eventually becomes bureaucracy. The routinization of charisma explains how fragile movements become enduring religions, but it also reveals the human mechanisms behind what is claimed as divine authority.

Émile Durkheim offered a complementary but more radical account. In The Elementary Forms of Religious Life, he argued that the sacred is not a supernatural reality but the collective power of society itself, misrecognized and symbolized in religious forms. When a community gathers in ritual, it experiences a surge of collective effervescence, a sense of being lifted beyond the individual into a larger whole. This experience is then projected outward as the presence of the sacred. The totem, the god, the holy text—these are symbols of the community's own power. Miracles, in this framework, are not violations of natural law but expressions of collective energy. Revelation is not divine speech but the articulation of communal values. Authority is not imposed from outside but generated by the group's own need for cohesion. Durkheim's analysis explains why religion persists even when its supernatural claims are undermined: it persists because it is society worshipping itself. The sacred is real, but it is social, not divine.

Later sociologists refined and extended these insights. Peter Berger argued that religion provides a "sacred canopy," a framework of meaning that shields individuals from the chaos of existence. In a world where death, suffering, and injustice threaten to overwhelm, religion offers a coherent narrative that makes sense of it all. Charles Taylor described religion as a "social imaginary," a way of inhabiting the world that cannot be replaced by secular institutions. Even in secular societies, Taylor argued, the longing for transcendence persists, and religious frameworks continue to shape moral and cultural life. These defenses of religion do not deny its social construction; they affirm it. Religion is powerful precisely because it constructs meaning, because it provides the canopy under which human life can flourish. Authority, in this view, is not a divine imposition but a human achievement, fragile yet indispensable.

Insider testimony complicates the sociological picture. Believers often describe authority as self authenticating, as something that compels obedience from within. A Catholic may describe papal authority as divinely instituted, while a Protestant may describe scriptural authority as self evident. A Muslim may describe the Qur'an as the direct speech of God, whose authority is undeniable. A Hindu may describe the Vedas as eternal, not authored by any human. A Buddhist may describe the Dharma as authoritative because it leads to liberation from suffering. These testimonies reflect not objective realities but communal constructions. Yet they cannot be dismissed as mere illusions. They are lived realities, shaping how people act, think, and feel. The sociologist must balance empathy with critique, recognizing both the constructedness of authority and its existential power.

Philosophical objections strike at the conceptual core. Hume's argument against miracles rests on the uniformity of nature: our experience of the world is governed by regular laws, and the weight of that uniform experience is always greater than the credibility of any testimony to the contrary. For Hume, extraordinary claims require extraordinary evidence, and miracle reports never meet this threshold. Even if multiple witnesses attest to a miracle, it is always more rational to assume deception, error, or exaggeration than to believe that the laws of nature have been suspended. This argument has been enormously influential, shaping modern skepticism toward miracle claims. Kant added another layer, arguing that miracles, even if they occurred, could never serve as the foundation of religion, because true religion must rest on moral reason, not on contingent events. Religion grounded in miracles is always vulnerable to doubt; religion grounded in morality is secure.

In the twentieth century, analytic philosophers questioned whether the very concept of a "violation of natural law" is coherent. Natural laws, they argued, are descriptive generalizations rather than prescriptive rules. To say that a miracle violates a law of nature is to misunderstand what a law of nature is. Postmodern thinkers like Derrida went further, suggesting that revelation itself is always mediated by language, and language is inherently unstable. There is no pure, unmediated divine speech; there are only texts, interpretations, and endless deferrals of meaning. Authority, therefore, is never absolute but always provisional, always subject to reinterpretation. Miracles, too, are caught in this play of signification: they are events only insofar as they are narrated, and narration is never innocent. Deconstruction does not deny the power of religion, but it denies its finality. Every claim to revelation is haunted by the possibility of alternative readings, every assertion of authority undermined by the instability of the text on which it rests.

Defenses have been mounted against these philosophical critiques. Alvin Plantinga has argued that belief in God and in divine action can be rational without evidence, because such beliefs are "properly basic," grounded in the same way that our trust in memory or perception is grounded. Richard Swinburne has contended that Hume's standard of evidence is too strict, and that cumulative testimony, especially when independent and consistent, can make belief in miracles rational. Jürgen Moltmann has reframed eschatological hope as a kind of miracle in history, not a violation of natural law but a sign of God's future breaking into the present. These defenses show that the philosophical debate is not closed. Yet they also reveal the limits of defense. Plantinga secures rationality for the believer but not persuasion for the skeptic. Swinburne's probabilistic calculus depends on prior theistic assumptions. Moltmann's theology inspires hope but does not resolve the epistemic problem. The defenses preserve faith, but they do not restore universal certainty.

Comparative traditions broaden the picture. In Judaism, the authority of Torah is often defended not by miracle claims but by the enduring covenantal relationship between God and Israel. The revelation at Sinai is remembered not as a violation of natural law but as the moment when a people entered into covenant. In Islam, the Qur'an is regarded not merely as a text but as the direct speech of God, whose authority is self authenticating. Its linguistic beauty, moral guidance, and transformative power are themselves evidence of its divine origin. In Hindu traditions, the Vedas are considered eternal, not authored by any human, and their authority is defended by their role in sustaining ritual and cosmic order. In Buddhism, the authority of the Dharma is defended not by appeal to miracles but by its pragmatic efficacy in reducing suffering and leading to enlightenment. Across traditions, the pattern repeats: authority is claimed, contested, and sustained through communal validation. Miracles and revelations function not as brute facts but as symbols of meaning, anchors of identity, and sources of cohesion.

What emerges from this dialectic is a pattern. The critiques—historical, psychological, sociological, philosophical—undermine the epistemic certainty of miracles, revelation, and authority. The defenses—whether probabilistic, existential, or theological—preserve their meaning for the faithful but cannot compel assent from the skeptic. The result is that religion cannot claim to offer indubitable proofs of divine intervention, but it can continue to offer symbols of hope, frameworks of meaning, and communities of belonging. Religion survives not because it has refuted its critics, but because it addresses dimensions of human existence that critique cannot exhaust.

The cumulative effect of the critiques is undeniable. Historical criticism has shown that sacred texts are human artifacts, stitched together from sources, shaped by editors, and embedded in cultural contexts. Psychological analysis has revealed that visions and revelations can be traced to the workings of the human mind, whether as projections of ideals, wish fulfillments, or altered states of consciousness. Sociological inquiry has demonstrated that authority is not a transparent channel of divine will but a social construction, generated and maintained by communities. Philosophical reflection has questioned whether the very concepts of miracle and revelation are coherent, whether they can bear the epistemic weight that has been placed upon them. Taken together, these critiques dismantle the traditional foundations of religious certainty. They show that miracles cannot serve as proofs, that revelation cannot function as unmediated divine speech, that authority cannot be grounded in unquestionable fiat.

And yet, religion persists. It persists not because these critiques are refuted, but because they do not exhaust the phenomenon they seek to explain. Religion is not merely a set of propositions about supernatural events. It is a way of life, a framework of meaning, a canvas on which human beings paint their deepest longings, fears, and hopes. To call religion a "mind painting" is to capture this paradox. Like a painting, religion is constructed, interpretive, and open to critique. It does not provide a photographic reproduction of reality; it offers a vision, a way of seeing. Its value lies not in empirical verification but in its capacity to orient human life, to inspire transformation, to sustain communities.

An informed reader may object that this conclusion reduces religion to illusion. If religion is a mind painting, does that not mean it is merely subjective, a projection with no claim to truth? But this objection rests on a narrow conception of truth. A painting is not true in the way a scientific proposition is true, but it can still be true in another sense: true to experience, true to the human condition, true to the search for meaning. Religion, like art, is not validated by correspondence to external fact but by its capacity to shape perception and evoke transformation. To say that religion is a mind painting is not to dismiss it as false; it is to recognize the mode of truth it embodies.

Another objection is that this conclusion leads to relativism. If all religions are mind paintings, are they all equally valid? Does this not collapse into a nihilism where anything goes? The answer is no, because paintings can still be evaluated. Some inspire compassion, others justify violence. Some open horizons of meaning, others close them down. The mind painting metaphor allows for evaluation without demanding epistemic certainty. Religions can be judged by their fruits, by the kinds of lives they foster, by the communities they sustain. The absence of indubitable proof does not mean the absence of criteria. It means that the criteria are existential and ethical rather than empirical.

A further objection is that this conclusion underestimates the resilience of faith. Believers will insist that miracles really happened, that revelation really is divine speech, that authority really is grounded in God. To them, the mind painting metaphor may seem like a betrayal. But the metaphor does not deny the sincerity of belief. It acknowledges that for the believer, the painting is not experienced as a painting but as reality itself. The power of religion lies precisely in this: that the constructed vision is lived as truth. The historian may expose the textual origins of miracles, the psychologist may trace the neural basis of revelation, the sociologist may reveal the social construction of authority, the philosopher may question the coherence of supernatural causality. Yet none of these critiques can erase the lived reality of faith. The painting is not diminished by being recognized as a painting; it is enriched, for we can then appreciate its artistry, its depth, its capacity to move and transform.

The metaphor also allows us to see why religion endures across cultures and traditions. In Judaism, the Torah functions as a mind painting of covenantal identity, a vision of a people bound to God through law and story. In Islam, the Qur'an is a mind painting of divine speech, a text whose beauty and power orient life toward submission to God. In Hinduism, the Vedas are mind paintings of cosmic order, sustaining ritual and dharma. In Buddhism, the Dharma is a mind painting of liberation, a path that reorients perception and desire. In Christianity, the Gospels are mind paintings of divine incarnation, narratives that shape communities around the figure of Christ. Each tradition constructs its own canvas, its own vision, its own way of seeing. None can claim epistemic certainty, but all can claim existential significance.

The academic attack, then, does not destroy religion; it clarifies the terms on which it survives. Religion cannot claim epistemic certainty in the face of historical, psychological, sociological, and philosophical critique. But it can claim existential significance. It can claim to be a form of art, a mind painting that shapes perception and sustains life. In this sense, the critiques are not threats but opportunities. They strip away illusions of certainty, forcing religion to confront its constructedness. But in doing so, they also reveal the depth of its power. For what is constructed can still be true in another sense: true to human experience, true to the search for meaning, true to the longing for transcendence.

The conclusion is not that religion is false, but that it is art. It is not a photograph of reality but a painting of meaning. It is not validated by proof but by its capacity to orient existence. To call religion a mind painting is to honor both its fragility and its power. It is fragile because it cannot withstand the demand for epistemic certainty; it is powerful because it continues to shape lives even without such certainty. Like a painting, it is open to interpretation, subject to critique, and vulnerable to dismissal. But also like a painting, it can inspire, transform, and endure. Religion is a human mind painting—constructed, contested, fragile, and yet enduring, because it continues to speak to the deepest needs of the human spirit.

Chapter Six
Morality Without the Divine

The question of whether ethical behavior requires divine foundation represents one of philosophy's most enduring and consequential debates, touching the deepest assumptions about human nature, moral obligation, and the source of normative authority. Religious traditions across cultures have long claimed exclusive or primary authority over moral guidance, asserting that without divine commandment, revelation, or spiritual grounding, human beings lack sufficient motivation, knowledge, or justification for ethical behavior. This claim demands rigorous examination not only because it affects billions of people who derive moral guidance from religious sources, but because it fundamentally challenges the possibility of secular ethical systems that could serve increasingly pluralistic societies where religious consensus no longer exists. The analysis that follows demonstrates that morality neither requires nor benefits from supernatural foundation, while acknowledging the legitimate psychological and social functions that religious moral frameworks currently serve for many communities worldwide.

The Euthyphro dilemma, first articulated in Plato's dialogue of the same name, poses the fundamental challenge to divine command theory that continues to generate philosophical debate over two millennia after its initial formulation. The dilemma presents theistic moral theorists with two seemingly unacceptable alternatives: either actions are morally good because God commands them, making morality arbitrary and dependent on divine whim, or God commands actions because they are already morally good, making divine commands irrelevant to moral truth and reducing God to a mere discoverer rather than creator of moral law. Sophisticated theological responses have emerged to address this challenge, but each attempted solution reveals additional problems that ultimately undermine the coherence of divine command approaches to ethics.

Divine command theorists typically respond to the Euthyphro dilemma by asserting that God's commands flow necessarily from God's perfectly good nature, avoiding both the arbitrariness problem (since God cannot command evil) and the irrelevance problem (since morality remains grounded in divine reality). William Alston's influential defense argues that divine goodness represents a distinct metaphysical category from moral obligation, allowing theists to maintain that God is morally good while avoiding the trivialization that would result if divine goodness merely meant conformity to divine commands. Robert Adams' modified divine command theory holds that ethical wrongness necessarily consists in being contrary to the commands of a loving God, making divine nature rather than arbitrary divine will the ultimate source of moral truth. These sophisticated formulations represent significant improvements over crude versions of divine command theory, but they fail to resolve fundamental problems with grounding morality in supernatural authority.

The most serious objection to modified divine command theory concerns the relationship between divine nature and moral truth that these approaches require. If God's nature is necessarily good, this necessity must be grounded in standards of goodness that exist independently of divine volition, undermining the claim that God creates or constitutes moral truth. Alternatively, if divine nature defines goodness tautologically, then assertions about divine moral perfection become analytically empty rather than providing substantive moral guidance. The attempted resolution through identifying God with goodness itself (rather than treating them as distinct concepts) faces the challenge of explaining how this identity relationship generates specific moral obligations that apply to finite human beings in particular historical circumstances. These theological maneuvers reveal that even sophisticated divine command theories cannot escape dependence on moral intuitions and rational reflection that operate independently of religious authority.

Furthermore, divine command approaches face insurmountable epistemological problems about identifying authentic divine communications and interpreting their moral implications. Religious traditions offer conflicting accounts of divine moral requirements, with no neutral theological method for resolving these disagreements. The historical record reveals that religious moral teachings have consistently reflected the cultural assumptions and social interests of their human interpreters rather than transcending these limitations through divine guidance. The moral progress that has occurred within religious traditions typically results from believers applying reason, empathy, and humanitarian concern to critique inherited teachings rather than from new divine revelations that correct previous moral errors. These patterns suggest that human moral reasoning provides the ultimate arbiter of religious moral claims rather than deriving its authority from supernatural sources.

Contemporary evolutionary approaches to ethics offer far more promising foundations for moral theory than divine command alternatives, despite legitimate concerns about deriving normative conclusions from descriptive evolutionary accounts. The is-ought problem, identified by David Hume and systematized by G.E. Moore, correctly identifies the logical gap between empirical descriptions of natural phenomena and normative prescriptions for human behavior. Simply describing how human moral psychology evolved through natural selection cannot by itself justify particular moral obligations or generate action-guiding principles for contemporary ethical decisions. However, this logical gap does not invalidate evolutionary approaches to ethics if they are formulated with appropriate attention to meta-ethical foundations and normative theory construction rather than naive attempts to read moral conclusions directly from biological facts.

The crucial insight involves recognizing that evolutionary accounts provide essential information about the psychological mechanisms underlying moral experience without determining the content of reflective moral judgment. Human beings possess evolved capacities for empathy, fairness, reciprocity, and concern for group welfare that make moral behavior psychologically possible, but the operation of these capacities in complex social environments requires rational reflection, cultural learning, and institutional development that extend far beyond automatic emotional responses. Evolutionary ethics succeeds when it explains the psychological preconditions that make moral behavior possible and attractive to human beings, rather than when it attempts to derive specific moral conclusions from biological premises alone.

Michael Shermer's approach to evolutionary ethics provides a promising framework for addressing the is-ought problem by grounding moral reasoning in the factual conditions required for human flourishing while acknowledging that flourishing itself represents a normative standard that requires philosophical justification. This approach begins with the empirical observation that human beings, as evolved organisms, possess species-specific needs and capacities that define the conditions under which they typically thrive. The normative component enters through the philosophical argument that rational agents have sufficient reason to promote conditions that enable flourishing for themselves and others, particularly given the social interdependence that characterizes human existence. This foundation provides substantive content for moral reasoning while avoiding the naturalistic fallacy through explicit acknowledgment of its normative commitments.

Cross-cultural anthropological research provides crucial support for evolutionary approaches to ethics by documenting remarkable consistency in basic moral concerns across diverse societies, while simultaneously revealing important cultural variations in how these concerns are prioritized and institutionalized. The Oxford anthropological study by Oliver Scott Curry and colleagues identified seven moral rules that appear universally across sixty cultures: help family members, help group members, return favors, be brave, defer to superiors, divide resources fairly, and respect others' property. These universal patterns strongly suggest evolutionary origins, as the specific combination of kin altruism, reciprocal cooperation, group solidarity, and resource management reflects the adaptive challenges that human ancestors faced in small-scale societies over hundreds of thousands of years.

However, the documentation of universal moral concerns should not obscure the substantial cultural variation in how societies elaborate, prioritize, and institutionalize these basic patterns. Western individualistic cultures tend to emphasize principles of individual rights, fairness, and personal autonomy, while Eastern collectivistic cultures place greater weight on loyalty, authority, and group harmony. These cultural differences reflect different strategies for organizing social cooperation under varying ecological, historical, and institutional conditions rather than fundamental disagreements about moral truth. The anthropological evidence supports a pluralistic universalism that recognizes common human moral capacities while respecting diverse cultural approaches to their development and expression.

The primate principle of amorality requires careful philosophical analysis to distinguish descriptive claims about evolved human psychology from normative conclusions about moral obligation. Evolutionary accounts of human behavior demonstrate that moral emotions and social preferences emerged through natural selection processes that favored individuals who could successfully navigate complex social environments through strategic cooperation, alliance formation, and reputation management. These evolved psychological mechanisms operate largely outside conscious awareness and continue influencing contemporary behavior through unconscious evaluation of social costs and benefits. Recognizing these evolutionary influences does not imply moral endorsement of strategic behavior or cynical dismissal of genuine moral motivation, but rather provides essential insight into the psychological factors that make moral behavior possible and appealing to human beings.

The descriptive account of human moral psychology reveals sophisticated mechanisms for social cooperation that operate through emotional systems (guilt, sympathy, gratitude, indignation) rather than conscious rational calculation. These emotional responses evolved because they typically promoted behaviors that enhanced reproductive success in ancestral environments, but their operation in contemporary contexts often generates genuine concern for others' welfare that extends far beyond narrow self-interest. The love that parents feel for children, the friendship bonds that develop through shared experiences, the compassion that motivates charitable behavior, and the sense of justice that drives political reform all reflect evolutionary inheritance, but this does not diminish their moral significance or reduce them to mere biological imperatives.

The normative implications of evolutionary psychology require careful philosophical development rather than direct derivation from biological premises. The fact that human beings possess evolved capacities for empathy, fairness, and cooperation provides essential information for constructing ethical theories that can successfully motivate moral behavior and create stable social institutions. Moral theories that conflict with fundamental features of human psychology are unlikely to generate widespread compliance or long-term social stability. However, understanding psychological constraints does not determine moral conclusions, as rational reflection can identify ways to extend, refine, and systematize evolved moral impulses that better serve human flourishing under contemporary conditions.

Secular humanism faces legitimate criticism for potential cultural ethnocentrism and Western bias that may limit its applicability across diverse cultural contexts. Traditional humanist manifestos have typically emerged from European Enlightenment traditions that emphasize individual autonomy, rational inquiry, and scientific progress as primary values, potentially overlooking moral insights from non-Western traditions that organize social life according to different principles. The emphasis on individual rights and personal freedom reflects particular historical experiences of Western societies rather than universal human values and imposing these priorities on cultures that emphasize communal solidarity, traditional authority, and spiritual transcendence risks perpetuating intellectual colonialism.

However, these legitimate concerns about cultural bias should not lead to complete relativistic abandonment of cross-cultural moral dialogue or universal human rights frameworks. The challenge involves developing secular ethical approaches that can incorporate insights from diverse moral traditions while maintaining commitment to principles that protect human dignity and promote social cooperation across cultural boundaries. Contemporary developments in comparative ethics demonstrate promising approaches for constructing inclusive moral frameworks that draw on global wisdom traditions rather than imposing Western philosophical categories on non-Western societies.

The integration of non-Western ethical traditions provides essential resources for developing more adequate secular moral frameworks that avoid the limitations of purely Western approaches. Ubuntu philosophy from Southern African traditions offers sophisticated insights about the relational nature of human identity and the importance of communal solidarity that complement and correct excessive Western individualism. The Ubuntu principle "umuntu ngumuntu ngabantu" (a person is a person through other people) provides philosophical foundation for understanding moral obligations as emerging from social relationships rather than abstract rational principles, while maintaining concern for individual dignity within communal contexts. Confucian ethical traditions contribute additional resources for understanding the cultivation of moral character through social roles, relationships, and institutional participation. Confucian emphasis on education, ritual practice, and hierarchical responsibility offers alternatives to Western contractual approaches to social organization, while Confucian concepts of jen (benevolence), li (ritual propriety), and wen (cultural refinement) provide substantive content for moral development that extends beyond procedural fairness or individual autonomy. The integration of Ubuntu relational insights with Confucian character development creates opportunities for secular ethical frameworks that address both individual flourishing and social harmony through attention to the cultural practices that shape moral experience.

Contemporary efforts to develop fusion approaches that combine insights from Western, African, and Asian traditions demonstrate the feasibility of constructing inclusive secular ethics that avoid cultural imperialism while maintaining normative content. These approaches typically emphasize shared human concerns (dignity, flourishing, cooperation, justice) while recognizing diverse cultural strategies for promoting these concerns through different institutional arrangements and social practices. The philosophical challenge involves identifying common ground across traditions without imposing artificial uniformity that obscures important cultural differences in moral reasoning and social organization.

Religious social benefits require balanced empirical assessment that acknowledges both positive and negative consequences of religious participation while avoiding selective attention to evidence that supports predetermined conclusions. Extensive longitudinal research demonstrates that regular religious participation correlates with numerous indicators of human flourishing: greater life satisfaction, stronger social relationships, better physical and mental health, higher levels of civic engagement, and reduced rates of substance abuse, depression, and suicide. These associations remain statistically significant even after controlling for demographic variables, socioeconomic status, and other factors that might explain the correlations through non-religious mechanisms.

However, interpreting these correlations requires careful attention to alternative explanations and potential negative consequences that may offset positive effects in particular circumstances. The social support provided by religious communities represents an important mechanism linking religious participation to wellbeing outcomes, but this mechanism operates through natural psychological and sociological processes rather than supernatural intervention. Other community organizations that provide similar social support, meaningful activities, and moral guidance might generate comparable benefits without requiring acceptance of supernatural beliefs or potentially divisive religious doctrines.

Religious communities also demonstrate concerning patterns of social exclusion, authoritarian control, resistance to moral progress, and justification of violence that must be weighed against positive contributions to human flourishing. Religious traditions have historically provided ideological support for slavery, patriarchal oppression, ethnic discrimination, scientific ignorance, and political authoritarianism, often resisting social reforms that later generations recognize as moral progress. Contemporary religious movements continue displaying these problematic tendencies through opposition to gender equality, LGBTQ rights, reproductive autonomy, and evidence-based education. These negative patterns suggest that religious social benefits may come at unacceptable costs for marginalized groups and social progress more generally.

The most promising approach involves identifying the specific features of religious communities that generate positive outcomes while determining whether secular alternatives could provide similar benefits without associated costs. Religious communities typically combine several elements that contribute to human flourishing: regular social interaction with stable groups, shared meaningful activities that transcend individual concerns, moral frameworks that provide guidance for difficult decisions, ritual practices that mark important life transitions, and institutional support during times of crisis or celebration. Secular organizations that successfully incorporate these features might achieve similar positive outcomes while avoiding supernatural commitments that create conflicts with scientific knowledge and moral reasoning.

The development of effective secular alternatives to religious community requires sustained attention to the psychological and social needs that religious participation currently addresses for billions of people worldwide. Simply criticizing religious beliefs without providing functional alternatives risks leaving people without essential resources for meaning-making, community belonging, and moral guidance that contribute significantly to human flourishing. The construction of secular institutions that can match the social benefits of religious communities while avoiding their problematic features represents one of the most important challenges for contemporary ethical theory and social policy.

Philosophical assessment of morality without the divine reveals that secular approaches to ethics possess superior theoretical foundations and greater potential for promoting human flourishing across diverse cultural contexts than religious alternatives. Evolutionary accounts of moral psychology provide more plausible explanations for the origins and universality of moral experience than supernatural revelation or divine command. Cross-cultural evidence demonstrates remarkable consistency in basic moral concerns that reflects shared evolutionary heritage rather than culturally specific religious teachings. The integration of insights from diverse wisdom traditions offers resources for developing inclusive secular ethics that avoid both Western cultural imperialism and uncritical moral relativism.

However, the practical success of secular morality depends not only on its theoretical adequacy but also on its ability to motivate widespread ethical behavior and create stable institutions that promote human cooperation across cultural boundaries. Religious traditions have demonstrated remarkable success in generating moral commitment, social solidarity, and institutional durability over extended historical periods. Secular alternatives must demonstrate comparable practical effectiveness while avoiding the intellectual and social costs associated with supernatural belief systems. This challenge requires innovative approaches to moral education, community organization, and cultural development that can engage human beings' deepest psychological needs while remaining consistent with scientific knowledge and rational moral reflection.

The ultimate conclusion supports neither the elimination of religious participation for individuals who find it personally meaningful nor the accommodation of religious authority in public policy decisions that affect diverse populations. Religious communities can continue serving important functions for their members while secular institutions develop alternative approaches that serve similar needs without requiring supernatural commitments. The goal involves creating social conditions where both religious and secular approaches to moral life can coexist and contribute to human flourishing, while maintaining that secular approaches possess superior intellectual foundations and greater potential for promoting justice across cultural differences. This nuanced position acknowledges the complexity of moral life while maintaining clear commitments about the sources of moral authority and the criteria for evaluating moral claims

Chapter Seven
Afterlife and Transcendence

The universal human preoccupation with death and the possibility of continued existence beyond bodily demise represents one of our species' most profound existential concerns, generating elaborate cultural systems that attempt to address mortality's challenge to meaning-making and social continuity. From the ancient Egyptian Book of the Dead to contemporary near-death experience narratives, from Buddhist concepts of rebirth to indigenous ancestor veneration, human societies have constructed remarkably diverse yet thematically consistent frameworks for understanding what happens when individual consciousness encounters the apparent finality of physical death. The anthropological analysis reveals that while beliefs about afterlife vary dramatically across cultures in their specific content and institutional expression, they consistently serve crucial psychological and social functions that transcend their empirical accuracy: providing comfort in the face of existential anxiety, maintaining social bonds beyond individual lifespans, establishing moral frameworks through posthumous accountability, and creating narrative continuity that bridges temporal limitations of individual experience.

Cross-cultural examination of immortality beliefs demands sophisticated analytical frameworks that avoid both reductionist dismissal of their cultural complexity and uncritical acceptance of their supernatural claims. The anthropological record demonstrates remarkable diversity in how societies conceptualize posthumous existence: some traditions emphasize personal continuity of individual consciousness (Christian heaven, Islamic paradise), others focus on cyclical transformation through reincarnation (Hindu samsara, Buddhist rebirth), while still others prioritize ancestral presence that continues influencing community life (African ancestral spirits, Confucian filial obligations). These variations reflect different cultural priorities about individuality, social relationships, moral responsibility, and cosmic order rather than representing competing empirical claims about objective posthumous realities.

The Fore people of Papua New Guinea exemplify sophisticated cultural approaches to posthumous existence that resist simple categorization as primitive superstition or religious delusion. The Fore practice of transumption—consuming deceased family members to ensure proper soul transition—emerges from complex beliefs about bodily continuity, ancestral presence, and social obligation that serve multiple functions simultaneously: maintaining spiritual connection between generations, encoding ecological wisdom about mortality and renewal, expressing profound respect for deceased individuals, and reinforcing kinship bonds through shared ritual participation. From the Fore perspective, Western burial practices appear cruel and spiritually destructive, trapping deceased individuals in isolated decay rather than facilitating their integration into ongoing community life through incorporation into living bodies.

The anthropological analysis reveals that afterlife beliefs consistently employ anthropomorphic projection to construct posthumous worlds that mirror familiar social relationships and cultural values rather than representing transcendent spiritual realities. Robert Hertz's influential analysis demonstrates that societies typically envision otherworldly existence as "analogous to ours, but more pleasant, and organized in the same way as it is here," suggesting that these beliefs function primarily as idealized extensions of current social arrangements rather than accurate descriptions of metaphysical realities. The Hungarian peasant tradition of feeding deceased souls through food steam and providing clothes for posthumous needs illustrates how afterlife beliefs anthropomorphize death by assuming continued material requirements that mirror living experience.

However, avoiding reductionist assumptions requires acknowledging that dismissing afterlife beliefs as mere psychological projection or cultural construction fails to engage seriously with their phenomenological significance for practitioners and their potential insights about consciousness, meaning, and human experience. Religious traditions often contain sophisticated philosophical frameworks for understanding the relationship between mind and body, individual and cosmos, temporal and eternal dimensions of existence that deserve respectful intellectual engagement regardless of their empirical accuracy about posthumous survival. The Tibetan Buddhist bardos, Islamic eschatology, Christian mystical traditions, and indigenous dreamtime concepts all provide complex theoretical resources for understanding consciousness, identity, and transcendence that extend beyond simple survival concerns.

Contemporary research on intuitive dualism provides crucial insights into the psychological mechanisms underlying universal afterlife beliefs while simultaneously challenging assumptions about their inevitability or accuracy. Jesse Bering's influential experimental work suggested that humans possess evolved cognitive biases toward mind-body dualism that make posthumous survival seem intuitively plausible, but more recent cross-cultural studies reveal a more complex picture. Cohen and colleagues' comprehensive analysis across six diverse populations demonstrates that while some psychological-continuity intuitions exist cross-culturally, most participants across all tested cultures do not actually exhibit strong dualist assumptions about posthumous mental state persistence. These findings suggest "intuitive materialism" as the default cognitive position, with dualist thinking representing a possible but not inevitable mode of reasoning about death and consciousness.

The cross-cultural evidence indicates that explicit afterlife beliefs often conflict with implicit psychological assumptions about mental state continuity after bodily death, suggesting that cultural transmission rather than evolved cognitive biases provides the primary mechanism driving afterlife belief systems. Religious education, ritual participation, authoritative teaching, and social reinforcement appear necessary to maintain supernatural beliefs about posthumous survival against natural psychological tendencies toward materialism about mind-brain relationships. This conclusion does not invalidate the cultural significance or personal meaning of afterlife beliefs, but it does clarify their origins in cultural learning rather than universal cognitive architecture.

The neurotheological approach to transcendent experiences provides valuable but limited insights into the biological mechanisms underlying spiritual states, religious visions, and near-death episodes that many practitioners interpret as evidence for afterlife realities. Andrew Newberg's pioneering SPECT imaging studies of Tibetan Buddhist monks and Franciscan nuns during peak meditative states reveal consistent patterns of brain activation: decreased activity in the posterior superior parietal lobe (associated with spatial self-orientation), increased activity in the prefrontal cortex (linked to focused attention), and altered neurotransmitter levels that correlate with reported experiences of ego dissolution, unity consciousness, and transcendent presence.

Near-death experience research demonstrates similar neurological patterns during episodes of clinical death, cardiac arrest, and related crisis states that many survivors interpret as evidence for consciousness survival beyond bodily death. Kevin Nelson's comprehensive analysis reveals that NDEs can be understood through well-established brain mechanisms: REM intrusion during consciousness transitions, temporal lobe activation generating religious imagery, endorphin release creating euphoric states, and memory consolidation processes that enhance the subjective reality of these experiences. The fact that NDEs feel "more real than real" to experiencers reflects normal properties of these neurological mechanisms rather than indicating supernatural causation or consciousness independence from brain function.

However, neurotheological findings must be situated as one perspective among many rather than providing definitive resolution to questions about consciousness, transcendence, and posthumous survival. The correlation between brain states and reported spiritual experiences cannot definitively determine the metaphysical status of these phenomena any more than identifying the neural correlates of music appreciation proves that musical beauty exists only in brain activity. The "hard problem of consciousness"—explaining how subjective experience emerges from objective physical processes—remains unsolved despite remarkable advances in neuroscientific understanding, counseling methodological humility about claims regarding consciousness, spirituality, and transcendence.

Moreover, reducing transcendent experiences to purely neurological phenomena risks overlooking their phenomenological richness, cultural significance, and potential insights about human consciousness that may not be captured through current scientific paradigms. The limitation of neurocentric models becomes particularly evident when considering that many transcendent experiences involve qualities—ineffability, noetic insight, unity consciousness, profound meaning—that resist easy translation into neurochemical descriptions. The challenge involves developing theoretical frameworks that can acknowledge both the neurological substrate of transcendent experiences and their irreducible phenomenological content without collapsing either dimension into the other.

Contemporary neuroscience research increasingly recognizes that consciousness poses fundamental explanatory challenges that purely reductionist approaches struggle to resolve. The recent Nature review by Cassol and colleagues acknowledges significant limitations in neurocentric models of near-death experiences, noting that current theories "omit key phenomenological features that are central to the core NDE experience and overextend beyond what the available evidence can support". This scientific humility opens space for integrating multiple perspectives—neurological, phenomenological, anthropological, and philosophical—in approaching questions about consciousness, transcendence, and posthumous possibilities.

Existentialist responses to mortality provide sophisticated philosophical frameworks for understanding human confrontation with finitude without requiring supernatural beliefs about posthumous survival. Martin Heidegger's analysis of "Being-toward-death" treats mortality not as a biological event to be feared or overcome, but as the fundamental structure that gives meaning and urgency to human existence. For Heidegger, authentic existence requires confronting one's own most possibility of death as the ultimate boundary that cannot be shared with others or indefinitely postponed, creating the temporal horizon within which life choices acquire genuine significance.

Heidegger's phenomenological approach reveals how everyday existence typically employs various strategies for avoiding direct confrontation with mortality: treating death as a distant statistical inevitability that happens to "anyone" rather than oneself, busying oneself with immediate concerns that obscure fundamental questions about existence, or adopting religious beliefs that promise escape from finitude through posthumous continuation. Authentic Being-toward-death involves abandoning these evasions and embracing mortality as the defining feature of human existence that makes individual choices meaningful precisely because they occur within finite temporal boundaries.

Karl Jaspers offers a complementary existential analysis that treats death as the most significant "boundary situation"—those limit experiences that confront individuals with the constraints and possibilities of human existence. Unlike Heidegger's focus on individual authenticity, Jaspers emphasizes how mortality challenges individuals to transcend their empirical limitations through connection with "Existenz"—the dimension of human being that points beyond finite temporal existence toward eternal significance. For Jaspers, facing death authentically does not require belief in personal immortality, but rather recognition that human existence participates in dimensions of meaning and value that transcend individual biological lifespans.

Søren Kierkegaard's pioneering existential analysis provides crucial insights into the anxiety and despair that characterize human confrontation with finitude, mortality, and the ultimate questions of existence. Kierkegaard identifies anxiety as the fundamental mood that arises from human freedom—the recognition that we must choose our existence without predetermined guidelines or guaranteed outcomes, including choices about how to understand and respond to our own mortality. This existential anxiety differs qualitatively from fear of specific objects or events; it represents the "dizziness of freedom" that emerges from confronting the radical openness of human existence within finite temporal boundaries.

For Kierkegaard, despair represents the deeper existential condition that results from failed attempts to construct stable identity and meaning within the constraints of finite existence. Despair emerges when individuals recognize the impossibility of achieving perfect synthesis between their finite limitations and infinite aspirations, their temporal existence and eternal longings. Unlike depression or sadness, despair represents a fundamental misalignment between one's authentic self and one's actual existence—a condition that can persist even during periods of apparent happiness or success.

Kierkegaard's analysis suggests that authentic existence requires embracing rather than eliminating the anxiety and despair that characterize human confrontation with mortality. Rather than seeking escape through religious promises of immortality or secular projects of meaning-creation, individuals must learn to live authentically within the tension between finite limitations and infinite aspirations that defines human existence. This existential maturity involves accepting uncertainty about ultimate questions while continuing to engage passionately with life's possibilities despite their temporal constraints.

Maurice Merleau-Ponty's phenomenological approach provides essential insights into how embodied existence shapes human understanding of mortality, transcendence, and the possibilities for meaning beyond individual biological lifespans. Merleau-Ponty's analysis of the lived body reveals how our experience of ourselves as embodied beings fundamentally structures all our engagements with the world, including our confrontation with mortality and finitude. The body functions not merely as a physical object among others, but as the primary medium through which consciousness encounters and makes sense of existence, including the ultimate boundary represented by death.

Merleau-Ponty's concept of "intercorporeality" illuminates how individual mortality occurs within networks of embodied relationships that can provide forms of transcendence without requiring supernatural beliefs about personal immortality. Through shared embodied experiences, cultural participation, and intersubjective meaning-creation, individuals participate in dimensions of human existence that extend beyond their particular biological lifespans. The phenomenology of grief reveals how bereaved individuals continue experiencing presence of deceased loved ones through embodied memories, shared practices, and cultural forms that preserve aspects of their relationships despite biological death.

This phenomenological analysis suggests that meaningful transcendence of individual mortality may occur through embodied participation in cultural traditions, social relationships, and creative expressions that outlast particular biological existences without requiring belief in personal consciousness survival. The embodied self extends beyond individual biological boundaries through its fundamental intertwining with other embodied beings and cultural practices that provide forms of continuation and significance that transcend individual death while remaining grounded in material existence.

Multiple philosophical voices contribute essential perspectives to understanding mortality and transcendence that avoid both naive religious literalism and reductive materialism. Albert Camus' analysis of the absurd reveals how human existence involves fundamental tension between our demand for meaning and purpose and the universe's apparent indifference to these demands, particularly evident in confrontation with mortality. Rather than resolving this tension through religious escape or philosophical rationalization, Camus advocates embracing the absurd condition while continuing to create values and meaning through passionate engagement with life despite its ultimate finitude.

Jean-Paul Sartre's existential analysis emphasizes how human consciousness involves fundamental "nothingness" that distinguishes us from other entities precisely through our capacity to negate, question, and transcend given circumstances. This "being-for-itself" creates both the possibility for authentic self-creation and the anxiety that comes from recognizing our radical freedom and responsibility, including responsibility for creating meaning in the face of mortality. For Sartre, death represents the ultimate boundary that gives urgency to human choices while revealing the groundlessness of human existence in any predetermined essence or purpose.

Contemporary existential psychology builds upon these philosophical foundations to develop therapeutic approaches that help individuals confront mortality anxiety, meaning-making challenges, and existential concerns without requiring religious beliefs about afterlife. Viktor Frankl's logotherapy emphasizes that meaning can be created through taking responsibility for one's response to unavoidable suffering, including the suffering that comes from recognizing human finitude and mortality. Irvin Yalom's existential therapy focuses on helping clients confront four ultimate concerns—death, freedom, isolation, and meaninglessness—as necessary steps toward authentic existence and psychological integration.

These therapeutic approaches demonstrate that individuals can develop psychologically healthy relationships with mortality and finitude without requiring supernatural beliefs about consciousness survival or posthumous existence. The existential framework provides resources for creating meaning, purpose, and transcendence within finite existence through authentic relationships, creative expression, ethical commitment, and acceptance of human limitations while continuing to engage passionately with life's possibilities.

The integration of anthropological, neurological, and philosophical perspectives reveals that while afterlife beliefs serve important psychological and social functions, they are not necessary for addressing existential concerns about mortality, meaning, and transcendence. Cross-cultural analysis demonstrates the remarkable diversity and cultural specificity of posthumous beliefs, suggesting their origins in particular social needs and cultural transmission rather than universal spiritual truths. Neuroscientific research illuminates the biological mechanisms underlying transcendent experiences without reducing their significance to purely physical processes. Existential philosophy provides sophisticated frameworks for creating meaning and confronting mortality within finite existence without requiring supernatural beliefs.

However, this analysis does not invalidate the personal significance or cultural value that afterlife beliefs provide for billions of individuals who find them meaningful and comforting. The goal involves understanding these beliefs sufficiently well to appreciate their functions while developing secular alternatives that can address similar psychological and social needs without requiring acceptance of empirically unsupported claims about consciousness survival or posthumous existence. This requires both intellectual rigor in evaluating truth claims and cultural sensitivity in recognizing the legitimate needs that afterlife beliefs currently serve for many communities worldwide.

The practical implications extend beyond academic debates to contemporary challenges in healthcare, end-of-life care, grief counseling, and public policy in increasingly secular societies. Healthcare professionals must navigate between respecting patients' religious beliefs about afterlife while providing evidence-based medical care and honest communication about prognosis and treatment options. Grief counselors need frameworks for supporting bereaved individuals that acknowledge their spiritual concerns while avoiding promotion of unfounded supernatural claims. Educational institutions require approaches to death education that can address existential concerns while maintaining commitment to scientific accuracy and cultural sensitivity.

The ultimate conclusion supports neither dogmatic rejection of all transcendent possibilities nor uncritical acceptance of traditional afterlife beliefs, but rather ongoing dialogue between scientific investigation, philosophical reflection, and cultural wisdom that can enhance human understanding of consciousness, mortality, and meaning within the constraints of available evidence. This approach maintains intellectual honesty about current limits of human knowledge while remaining open to insights from diverse cultural traditions and ongoing scientific discoveries that may deepen understanding of consciousness, transcendence, and the possibilities for meaning beyond individual biological existence.

Chapter Eight
Institutions, Power, and Social Control

Religious institutions exercise power through complex networks that extend far beyond overt coercion or simple authoritarian control. Understanding how religious authority functions requires engaging with sophisticated theoretical frameworks that illuminate the subtle, pervasive mechanisms through which institutions shape believers' subjectivity, normalize particular worldviews, and generate compliance through internalized discipline rather than external force. Michel Foucault's groundbreaking analysis of power/knowledge relationships reveals how modern institutions produce "subjects" whose desires, moral commitments, and self-understanding align with institutional objectives through dispersed technologies of normalization, surveillance, and self-regulation. Max Weber's typology of legitimate authority—traditional, charismatic, and rational-legal—provides essential tools for analyzing how religious organizations achieve legitimacy and maintain compliance across diverse cultural contexts. Ethnographic case studies from contemporary religious communities demonstrate how these theoretical insights operate in practice, revealing both the effectiveness of institutional power and the creative ways believers negotiate, resist, and transform authoritative structures.

However, these analytical approaches face legitimate philosophical challenges: critics argue that Foucaultian analysis risks excessive structuralism that overlooks individual agency and spiritual authenticity, while Weberian typologies may oversimplify the fluid dynamics of religious authority. Additionally, ethnographic representation requires careful attention to ethical issues about scholarly power, cultural sensitivity, and community self-determination that demand ongoing methodological reflection.

Michel Foucault's concept of disciplinary power illuminates how religious institutions exercise authority through subtle mechanisms that shape believers' subjectivity without requiring overt coercion or violence. In Discipline and Punish and The History of Sexuality, Foucault demonstrates how modern institutions—prisons, hospitals, schools, and military organizations—produce compliant subjects through practices of surveillance, normalization, examination, and self-regulation that make external force largely unnecessary. Religious institutions employ analogous techniques: seminary training programs inculcate future clergy with doctrinal frameworks that define legitimate belief and practice; catechetical curricula shape laypeople's moral imagination through systematic instruction in approved interpretations; liturgical calendars structure temporal consciousness so that religious observance becomes habitual; confessional practices train believers to monitor and report their own moral lapses; and pastoral counseling normalizes institutional guidance for personal decision-making. These dispersed practices operate together as what Foucault terms an "apparatus" of power/knowledge—not an external imposition but an internalized grid that organizes believers' experience of themselves, their relationships, and their moral obligations.

The genealogy of Christian disciplinary practices reveals striking continuities between monastic techniques and modern institutional control. Foucault traces how medieval monasteries developed sophisticated technologies of spiritual discipline: detailed regulation of daily activities, constant supervision by spiritual directors, systematic examination of conscience, and ritualized confession that required exhaustive self-scrutiny. These monastic innovations created what Foucault calls "a political anatomy of detail"—comprehensive attention to minute aspects of behavior, thought, and desire that rendered subjects transparent to institutional surveillance while generating forms of self-knowledge that aligned personal identity with institutional norms. The Qumran community's Community Rule provides an ancient example of such disciplinary mechanisms, prescribing elaborate punishments for violations of community standards and requiring members to participate in their own surveillance through mutual monitoring and reporting. Contemporary religious institutions employ similar techniques: evangelical accountability partnerships, Catholic examination of conscience, Islamic daily prayers that structure temporal consciousness, and Buddhist meditation practices that cultivate self-observation all function as disciplinary technologies that produce subjects who regulate themselves according to institutional norms.

However, Foucault's analysis faces legitimate criticism for potentially reducing all religious phenomena to expressions of power while overlooking genuine spiritual experience, individual agency, and the possibility of authentic transcendence that believers report. Critics argue that emphasizing power/knowledge relationships risks what they term "excessive structuralism"—analytical frameworks that flatten the rich diversity of devotional life into mechanistic accounts of social control, ignoring both the phenomenological reality of religious experience and believers' capacity for creative resistance, reinterpretation, and spiritual innovation. To address these concerns, it is essential to distinguish between Foucault's descriptive project—revealing how power circulates through knowledge production—and normative evaluations that either celebrate or condemn particular institutional arrangements. Foucault did not deny individual agency; rather, he demonstrated how agency emerges within power relations and how subjects can appropriate, subvert, or resist institutional regimes through what he terms "counter-conduct"—creative practices that deploy institutional resources for purposes that exceed or challenge official objectives.

The phenomenon of lay mysticism within Catholic traditions exemplifies such counter-conduct, as individual believers have historically challenged clerical authority by asserting direct spiritual access to divine reality that bypasses institutional mediation. Figures like Meister Eckhart, Julian of Norwich, and Teresa of Avila developed vernacular theological vocabularies, private devotional practices, and mystical experiences that reconfigured official liturgies and doctrinal formulations while remaining technically within orthodox boundaries. Contemporary examples include liberation theology's reinterpretation of scripture through lenses of social justice, Pentecostal movements that emphasize direct spiritual experience over clerical expertise, and feminist theological scholarship that challenges patriarchal institutional structures while drawing on traditional spiritual resources. These cases demonstrate that Foucaultian analysis can illuminate both domination and resistance, capturing the dynamic interplay between institutional power and personal spirituality without reducing either dimension to the other.

Max Weber's foundational analysis of legitimate authority provides complementary theoretical tools for understanding how religious institutions achieve compliance and maintain organizational stability across diverse cultural contexts. Weber identifies three "pure types" of legitimate domination that operate within religious organizations: traditional authority relies on inherited customs and sacred precedents; charismatic authority emerges from perceived extraordinary qualities of religious leaders; and rational-legal authority grounds legitimacy in codified rules, bureaucratic procedures, and professional expertise. Traditional authority manifests in hereditary priesthoods, established liturgical practices, apostolic succession claims, and scriptural traditions that derive legitimacy from antiquity and continuity with sacred origins. Charismatic authority appears in prophetic movements, mystical teachers, revivalist preachers, and spiritual innovators whose personal magnetism attracts devoted followers who recognize their exceptional spiritual gifts. Rational-legal authority characterizes modern denominations with professional clergy training, bureaucratic hierarchies, systematic theology, and administrative structures that operate according to codified procedures rather than personal relationships or traditional customs.

Weber emphasizes that empirical religious institutions invariably combine these ideal types in complex hybrid arrangements rather than manifesting pure forms. The Catholic Church, for example, simultaneously claims traditional authority through apostolic succession, incorporates charismatic elements through saint veneration and mystical traditions, and employs rational-legal structures through canon law, seminary education, and hierarchical administration. Protestant denominations typically emphasize rational-legal authority through democratic governance and professional ministerial training while maintaining traditional authority through scriptural interpretation and incorporating charismatic elements through evangelical conversion experiences. Islamic institutions balance traditional authority derived from Quranic revelation and prophetic example with rational-legal structures of Islamic jurisprudence and charismatic authority embodied in Sufi masters and contemporary religious innovators.

Reconciling divergent interpretations of Weber requires acknowledging both his ideal-type analytical method and the historical contingency of real-world institutions. Some scholars emphasize Weber's normative concern with rationalization as creating an "iron cage" of bureaucratic formalism that threatens to eliminate charismatic creativity and traditional wisdom from religious life. Others highlight Weber's recognition of charisma's enduring potential for renewal within institutional contexts, noting how charismatic movements can revitalize traditional structures and how rational-legal frameworks can facilitate rather than constrain spiritual innovation. Weber himself recognized that charismatic authority faces inherent instability because it depends on followers' continued recognition of the leader's extraordinary qualities, making "routinization of charisma" through traditional or rational-legal structures necessary for institutional survival. However, this routinization process creates ongoing tension between the spontaneous creativity that characterizes charismatic movements and the predictable procedures required for organizational stability.

A balanced Weberian analysis examines how religious institutions navigate these tensions through dynamic processes that combine stability and transformation. The early Christian church illustrates this process: Jesus' charismatic authority became routinized through apostolic succession (traditional) and ecclesiastical organization (rational-legal), but periodic charismatic renewal movements—monasticism, mysticism, reformation, revivalism—have repeatedly challenged institutional crystallization. Similarly, Islamic history demonstrates how the Prophet Muhammad's charismatic authority became institutionalized through caliphate succession and sharia jurisprudence, while Sufi orders, reformist movements, and contemporary Islamic renewal demonstrate ongoing charismatic vitality within traditional and rational-legal frameworks. Contemporary Pentecostalism provides another example: founding charismatic experiences become denominational structures with professional clergy and administrative hierarchies, yet individual congregations maintain space for spontaneous spiritual manifestations that can challenge or revitalize institutional routines.

Ethnographic case studies provide essential empirical grounding for theoretical analysis, revealing how local communities experience, negotiate, and sometimes resist institutional power and authority in their daily religious lives. The Sikh gurdwara in Yuba City, California, demonstrates how religious institutions serve multiple functions simultaneously: spiritual community, cultural preservation, social service provision, and civic engagement training. The gurdwara operates through the principle of seva (selfless service) that requires community members to participate in food preparation, facility maintenance, and charitable activities that extend beyond the religious community to serve broader social needs. This institutional structure generates forms of social capital that enable community members to develop civic leadership skills: several gurdwara participants have successfully entered local politics, drawing on organizational experience and community networks developed through religious participation. The case illustrates how religious authority operates through voluntary participation in meaningful activities rather than coercive control, while simultaneously demonstrating how institutional involvement shapes participants' civic identity and political engagement.

However, representing such communities ethically requires careful attention to practitioners' own interpretations of their religious life and avoiding analytical frameworks that reduce their spiritual commitments to merely social or political functions. Sikh participants emphasize that seva represents genuine spiritual practice rather than strategic civic training, and they understand gurdwara participation as religious obligation rather than instrumental social networking. Ethnographers must foreground these emic perspectives while maintaining analytical distance that can illuminate social patterns that participants may not consciously recognize. This methodological challenge requires what organizational ethnography scholars call "destabilizing the insider/outsider binary" through collaborative research relationships that treat community members as intellectual partners rather than passive research subjects.

The Religious Society of Friends (Quakers) provides another instructive ethnographic example of how distinctive decision-making practices embody particular forms of religious authority. The Quaker business method operates through collective discernment processes that seek spiritual guidance rather than majority rule or hierarchical command. Meeting participants sit in contemplative silence until individuals feel moved by the Spirit to offer insights, concerns, or proposals that contribute to communal wisdom. Decisions emerge through gradual consensus that reflects the meeting's sense of spiritual leading rather than through formal voting or executive authority. This process illustrates Weber's concept of charismatic authority operating through collective rather than individual manifestation: the group as a whole seeks access to divine guidance that transcends human reasoning or institutional procedure.

Ethnographic study of Quaker decision-making reveals both the distinctive spiritual dimensions of this practice and its practical organizational effectiveness. Participants report that the business method generates decisions that feel spiritually grounded and communally owned, creating stronger commitment to implementation than procedures based on majority rule or executive authority. However, the process requires significant time investment, high levels of trust among participants, and shared commitment to Quaker spiritual principles that may limit its applicability in more diverse religious contexts. The ethnographic analysis demonstrates how religious authority can operate through horizontal rather than vertical relationships while maintaining institutional coherence and decision-making capacity.

Contemporary Pentecostal movements in Kerala, India, provide a third ethnographic example that illuminates how global religious institutions adapt to local cultural contexts through creative negotiations of traditional, charismatic, and rational-legal authority. Pentecostal churches attract marginalized Dalit communities through highly participatory worship practices, economic assistance programs, and healing rituals that address daily hardships within Indian social contexts. Transnational denominational networks provide theological frameworks, training materials, and financial resources that standardize certain aspects of religious practice, while local pastors adapt sermons, prayers, and pastoral care to address caste discrimination, gender violence, and economic precarity specific to Kerala contexts.

The ethnographic evidence reveals how Pentecostal authority operates through multiple mechanisms simultaneously: traditional authority derived from biblical scripture and apostolic tradition; charismatic authority manifested through spiritual gifts, healing practices, and ecstatic worship; and rational-legal authority embodied in denominational structures, clergy training programs, and international organizational networks. Local believers creatively appropriate these different authority sources to address their particular social needs while maintaining connections to global Pentecostal identity. The case demonstrates both the adaptability of religious institutions and the agency of local communities in shaping how institutional authority operates within their cultural contexts.

However, representing Kerala Pentecostalism ethically requires avoiding both romanticized portrayals of grassroots agency and patronizing assumptions about religious manipulation or false consciousness. Dalit participants understand their religious involvement as genuine spiritual conversion that provides access to divine power, social dignity, and community belonging that extend beyond instrumental calculations about material advantage. Simultaneously, the ethnographic analysis can illuminate how Pentecostal practices function to address social inequalities and provide alternative forms of authority that challenge traditional Hindu caste hierarchies without reducing believers' spiritual commitments to merely social or political motivations. This analytical balance requires methodological approaches that respect practitioners' religious self-understanding while maintaining critical examination of how religious institutions operate within broader social power relationships.

Latin American liberation theology movements provide additional ethnographic examples of how religious communities can appropriate institutional authority for purposes that challenge rather than reinforce existing social hierarchies. In El Salvador, Brazil, Nicaragua, and other contexts, Catholic base communities reinterpret official Vatican teachings through lenses of social justice and political solidarity with impoverished populations. Biblical exegesis becomes a tool for social analysis: interpretations of Exodus narratives legitimate resistance to oppressive government policies, readings of prophetic literature support land reform movements, and Gospel teachings about "God's preferential option for the poor" provide theological foundations for challenging economic inequality. These communities leverage traditional authority (scriptural interpretation), rational-legal authority (theological scholarship, university positions), and charismatic authority (prophetic witness, martyrdom) to legitimize grassroots resistance while maintaining formal membership within institutional Catholicism.

The liberation theology case illustrates Foucault's concept of power's "reversibility"—how institutional resources can be appropriated for counter-hegemonic purposes that exceed or challenge official objectives. Base communities use Catholic social teaching, theological education, and ecclesiastical networks to support political movements that Vatican leadership often opposes, demonstrating how religious authority can be contested terrain rather than simple top-down control. However, this appropriation occurs within institutional constraints: liberation theologians face censure from conservative church hierarchies, state persecution from military governments, and ongoing pressure to moderate their political involvement. The ethnographic evidence reveals both the possibilities and limitations of resistance within institutional religious contexts.

Representing liberation theology communities ethically requires sensitivity to the dangers participants face from both religious and political authorities, collaborative research methodologies that share benefits with communities rather than extracting data for academic purposes, and reflexive analysis of the ethnographer's own positionality within global power relationships. Researchers from wealthy countries studying impoverished religious communities must acknowledge how academic careers depend on research access while community members risk persecution for their political involvement. Ethical ethnographic practice requires long-term commitment, reciprocal relationships, and research designs that serve community needs rather than merely academic advancement.

The Yoruba religious practices in southwestern Nigeria provide a final ethnographic example that challenges Western assumptions about religious boundaries and institutional coherence. Yoruba practitioners routinely participate in Ifá divination systems, Christian churches, and Islamic communities simultaneously, creating plural religious fields where different forms of authority operate according to different logics for different purposes. Ifá divination provides guidance for daily decision-making through cowrie shell readings interpreted by trained diviners who claim access to Orunmila's wisdom. Christian worship offers community fellowship, moral instruction, and participation in global religious networks. Islamic practices provide additional spiritual resources, educational opportunities, and connections to broader West African Muslim communities.

Ethnographic analysis reveals that Yoruba practitioners see no fundamental contradiction among these different religious involvements, situating them within broader cosmological frameworks that accommodate multiple sources of spiritual authority. The concept of àṣẹ (divine force or energy) operates across different religious contexts, while ethical principles like ìwà pẹ̀lẹ́ (gentle character) provide integrative frameworks that transcend particular institutional boundaries. This religious ecology challenges analytical frameworks that assume mutually exclusive religious commitments or that treat "syncretism" as cultural contamination rather than creative appropriation.

Representing Yoruba religious practices ethically requires avoiding both exoticizing portrayals that emphasize cultural difference and reductive analyses that treat complex spiritual traditions as primitive survivals or strategic adaptations to modernity. Yoruba cosmological concepts deserve respectful engagement as sophisticated intellectual achievements rather than objects for Western analytical translation. Ethnographers must learn indigenous languages, engage with traditional knowledge holders as intellectual authorities, and develop collaborative research relationships that acknowledge Yoruba practitioners as theorists of their own religious experience rather than passive subjects of external analysis.

The integration of Foucaultian power analysis, Weberian authority typologies, and ethnographic case studies reveals that religious institutions exercise social control through multiple overlapping mechanisms rather than simple authoritarian domination. Disciplinary power operates through normalization processes that shape believers' subjectivity, while legitimate authority emerges through traditional customs, charismatic leadership, and rational-legal procedures that generate voluntary compliance. Ethnographic evidence demonstrates both the effectiveness of institutional power and the creative ways believers negotiate, resist, and transform authoritative structures to address local needs and express spiritual authenticity. However, this analysis must be defended against charges of excessive structuralism by acknowledging individual agency, spiritual experience, and the possibilities for counter-conduct within institutional contexts. Weberian typologies require recognition of their ideal-type character and attention to the fluid dynamics of real-world religious authority. Ethnographic representation demands methodological reflexivity, collaborative research relationships, and ethical sensitivity to community self-determination and cultural autonomy.

The theoretical and empirical insights developed in this chapter provide essential tools for understanding how religious institutions maintain their enduring influence in human societies through sophisticated mechanisms of power and social control that extend far beyond overt coercion. Religious authority operates through the production of subjects who internalize institutional norms, the cultivation of legitimate authority through traditional, charismatic, and rational-legal means, and the creative adaptation of institutional resources by local communities who appropriate religious authority for their own purposes. Understanding these processes is crucial for any comprehensive analysis of religion's social and political functions in contemporary global contexts, where religious institutions continue playing significant roles in shaping individual identity, community solidarity, and political mobilization across diverse cultural settings.

Chapter Nine
Violence, Conflict, and Boundary-Making

Religious violence represents one of humanity's most persistent and complex phenomena, challenging simple explanations that attribute conflict either solely to theological differences or exclusively to material factors. The relationship between religious belief and violent behavior demands sophisticated analysis that avoids both reductionist materialism that dismisses religious motivations as mere cover for political interests and essentialist approaches that treat certain religious traditions as inherently violent. Contemporary scholarship reveals that religious conflicts emerge from complex interactions between theological narratives, social identity formation, economic competition, political mobilization, and historical grievances that resist monocausal explanations. Understanding religious violence requires examining how sacred narratives become weaponized through processes of boundary-making that transform theological differences into existential threats, while simultaneously acknowledging the legitimate grievances, material conditions, and political dynamics that provide fertile ground for religious mobilization. This analysis must defend against several predictable objections: accusations of reductionism from religious practitioners who emphasize theological authenticity, charges of false equivalence from critics who argue that some traditions are more violent than others, and post-secular critiques that challenge the secular-religious distinction underlying much academic analysis.

The anthropological and historical record demonstrates that virtually every major religious tradition has both sanctioned violence and provided resources for peacemaking, suggesting that the capacity for both conflict and reconciliation lies not in specific theological doctrines but in how religious communities interpret their traditions under particular social and political circumstances. Christianity sanctified the Crusades, Inquisition, and colonial conquest while simultaneously inspiring movements for social justice, nonviolent resistance, and humanitarian aid. Islam has provided ideological frameworks for both jihadist militancy and interfaith dialogue, both sectarian warfare and peaceful coexistence between Sunni and Shia communities. Buddhism, despite its emphasis on compassion and nonviolence, has supported ethnic cleansing in Myanmar against Rohingya Muslims and nationalist violence in Sri Lanka against Tamil minorities. Hinduism has inspired both Gandhi's nonviolent independence movement and contemporary Hindu nationalism that targets religious minorities. Judaism has produced both prophetic traditions emphasizing justice and peace and militant movements that justify violence against Palestinians through theological interpretations of land and covenant.

These patterns reveal that religious violence emerges not from essential theological characteristics but from how religious traditions become entangled with ethnic identity, territorial disputes, political competition, and social stratification in ways that transform theological differences into group conflicts over material resources and political power. The key analytical insight involves understanding how religious narratives provide symbolic resources for articulating group boundaries, legitimizing political claims, and mobilizing collective action, while simultaneously examining the underlying social conditions that make such mobilization appealing to particular populations. This approach avoids the trap of treating religion as either purely epiphenomenal or causally primary, instead examining how religious and material factors interact in specific historical contexts to produce violent outcomes.

Historical case studies illustrate the complexity of religious conflict and the inadequacy of monocausal explanations. The Thirty Years' War (1618-1648) in Europe is often cited as a paradigmatic religious conflict between Protestant and Catholic powers, but detailed historical analysis reveals that the war's origins, conduct, and resolution involved complex interactions between theological disputes, dynastic competition, territorial ambitions, trade rivalries, and state-building projects that resist simple religious/secular categorization. While religious differences provided ideological justification for warfare and shaped alliance patterns, material interests drove strategic decisions, and the war's conclusion through the Peace of Westphalia established principles of state sovereignty and religious coexistence that subordinated theological concerns to political stability. Similarly, the French Wars of Religion (1562-1598) involved genuine theological conflicts between Catholics and Huguenots, but these religious divisions became entangled with noble factional struggles, urban-rural tensions, foreign interventions, and crown weakness in ways that transformed doctrinal disputes into comprehensive social warfare.

Contemporary religious conflicts display similar complexity. The Israeli-Palestinian conflict involves genuine religious dimensions—competing claims to sacred sites, theological narratives about divine promises, and religious symbolism that shapes group identity—but attempts to explain the conflict primarily through religious differences ignore the central roles of nationalism, territorial displacement, economic inequality, military occupation, and geopolitical competition. Palestinian Christians participate in resistance to Israeli occupation alongside Palestinian Muslims, while secular Israeli Jews support settlement expansion alongside religious Zionists, indicating that religious and secular motivations overlap rather than form distinct causal categories. The conflict's persistence reflects not irreconcilable theological differences but political dynamics involving state formation, resource control, demographic anxiety, and regional power struggles that use religious symbolism to mobilize support and legitimize claims.

The Northern Ireland conflict provides another instructive example of how religious identity becomes entangled with ethnic nationalism, economic competition, and political exclusion in ways that transform theological differences into violent confrontation. While Protestant and Catholic theological differences provided symbolic resources for group identification, the conflict's roots lay in colonial settlement patterns, economic discrimination, political exclusion, and competing national loyalties that made religious identity coincide with social position and political allegiance. The Good Friday Agreement's success in ending most violence depended not on resolving theological disputes but on creating political institutions that accommodated competing national identities while providing mechanisms for power-sharing and addressing economic grievances.

Nigerian conflicts between Christian and Muslim communities illustrate how religious differences become activated by competition over political resources, land rights, and economic opportunities in ways that transform local disputes into religious warfare. The expansion of Fulani pastoralism into Middle Belt farming areas creates conflicts over grazing rights and agricultural land that become interpreted through religious lenses because pastoral communities are predominantly Muslim while farming communities are predominantly Christian. Population growth, climate change, urbanization, and competition for government resources exacerbate these tensions by intensifying competition over scarce resources while weak state institutions fail to provide effective dispute resolution mechanisms. Religious leaders and politicians exploit these tensions by framing local conflicts in cosmic terms that mobilize wider religious communities and justify violent responses to perceived threats.

Defending against monocausal explanations requires acknowledging both the genuine role that religious beliefs play in motivating violence and the complex social conditions that make religious mobilization effective. Religious narratives provide powerful resources for understanding suffering, identifying enemies, justifying violence, and promising ultimate vindication that secular ideologies often lack. Theological concepts of sacred warfare, divine justice, martyrdom, and cosmic struggle offer transcendent meaning for violent sacrifice that purely political or economic motivations cannot match. However, these religious resources become activated and sustained by social conditions—group threat, economic competition, political exclusion, historical grievances—that create receptive audiences for religious mobilization. The most intense religious conflicts typically occur where religious differences overlap with ethnic boundaries, economic inequalities, political exclusion, and territorial disputes in ways that make religious identity coincide with material interests.

Tribal storytelling and identity politics represent crucial mechanisms through which religious differences become transformed into group conflicts that justify violence against religious others. Religious communities develop narrative frameworks that define group boundaries, establish moral obligations, interpret historical experiences, and anticipate future destiny in ways that can either promote peaceful coexistence or legitimate violent confrontation with outsiders. These narratives operate through what social psychologists term "pseudospeciation"—the process by which groups define themselves as fundamentally different from and superior to other human groups, treating outsiders as less than fully human and therefore legitimate targets for violence. Religious traditions provide particularly powerful resources for pseudo speciation because they offer ultimate explanations for group difference, divine sanction for group superiority, and cosmic significance for group survival.

The construction of religious identity involves selective interpretation of sacred texts, historical memories, and contemporary experiences that emphasize group uniqueness, moral superiority, and existential threat from religious others. This process requires what Benedict Anderson terms "imagined community" formation—the creation of shared identity among people who will never meet but who understand themselves as members of a bounded group with common destiny. Religious communities develop elaborate mythologies about their origins, special relationship with the divine, historical persecution, and ultimate vindication that create emotional bonds and moral obligations among believers while establishing clear boundaries between insiders and outsiders.

However, distinguishing between narrative causality and material factors requires careful analysis of how storytelling interacts with social conditions to produce violent outcomes. Religious narratives provide frameworks for interpreting material conditions rather than creating conflicts independently of social circumstances. Economic inequality, political exclusion, territorial displacement, and social marginalization create grievances that religious narratives help interpret and address, but these narratives become persuasive only when they correspond to lived experiences of injustice, threat, or humiliation. The most effective religious mobilization occurs when theological explanations align with material realities in ways that make religious identity appear to be the most relevant framework for understanding and responding to social problems.

Ethnic boundary-making theory provides essential insights into how religious identity becomes politically salient and potentially violent. Andreas Wimmer's influential analysis demonstrates that ethnic boundaries emerge through strategic interactions between actors who compete to define group membership, establish boundary meanings, and mobilize collective action. Religious boundaries operate similarly, with religious leaders, political entrepreneurs, and community activists competing to define authentic religious identity, interpret theological traditions, and mobilize believers for collective action. These boundary-making processes involve three key strategies: boundary shifting (redefining who counts as a group member), boundary blurring (reducing the salience of group distinctions), and boundary crossing (changing individual group membership). Religious conflicts intensify when boundary-making strategies emphasize exclusion, purification, and mobilization while de-emphasizing accommodation, integration, and individual choice.

The institutional framework within which boundary-making occurs significantly influences whether religious differences generate conflict or coexistence. Political systems that recognize multiple religious communities, provide representation for religious minorities, and create incentives for cross-cutting alliances tend to moderate religious conflict by making religious identity less politically relevant. Constitutional arrangements that establish religious freedom, separate religious and political authority, and protect minority rights create institutional contexts where religious differences need not become zero-sum political competitions. Conversely, political systems that privilege particular religious communities, exclude religious minorities from political participation, or make religious identity the primary basis for political mobilization create incentives for religious conflict by making religious boundaries coincide with political access.

Economic structures also influence religious boundary-making by determining whether religious identity correlates with material advantage or disadvantage. Religious conflicts intensify when religious communities occupy different positions in economic hierarchies, compete for scarce resources, or experience differential impacts from economic changes. The overlap of religious and class boundaries creates conditions where economic grievances become interpreted through religious lenses while religious mobilization provides resources for addressing material concerns. Religious violence often emerges when economically marginalized communities use religious identity to challenge existing hierarchies while economically privileged groups use religious justifications to defend their advantages.

Contemporary research on tribal citizenship among Native American nations provides instructive parallels for understanding how identity boundaries become contested sites where cultural authenticity, political rights, and material resources intersect. Native nations use varying criteria for determining tribal membership—blood quantum, lineal descent, tribal rolls, cultural participation—that reflect different strategies for maintaining cultural identity while managing demographic pressures, economic resources, and political autonomy. These boundary-making processes involve tensions between inclusive approaches that emphasize cultural participation and exclusive approaches that emphasize genetic inheritance, with significant implications for access to tribal services, political representation, and cultural preservation. The colonial origins of blood quantum criteria illustrate how external impositions become internalized and reproduced through institutional mechanisms that shape contemporary identity politics.

Religious communities face analogous challenges in defining authentic membership, maintaining theological integrity, and managing resource allocation in contexts of cultural change, demographic pressure, and external challenge. Orthodox Judaism's debates over conversion standards, Catholic discussions of communion eligibility, Islamic controversies over sectarian boundaries, and Protestant disputes over doctrinal requirements reflect similar tensions between inclusive and exclusive approaches to religious identity. These boundary-making processes have significant implications for interfaith relations, as exclusive approaches tend to emphasize religious differences and legitimate separation while inclusive approaches facilitate dialogue and cooperation across religious lines.

The suppression of contradictory evidence represents a crucial mechanism through which religious communities maintain narrative coherence and group solidarity in the face of disconfirming information. Religious violence often involves systematic efforts to eliminate alternative interpretations, silence dissenting voices, and destroy evidence that challenges dominant group narratives. This suppression occurs through multiple mechanisms: censoring religious texts that support peaceful interpretations, marginalizing religious leaders who advocate interfaith dialogue, destroying historical evidence that contradicts group mythology, and punishing community members who question official narratives. The methodological challenge for scholars involves developing transparent approaches that can document these suppression mechanisms without reproducing them through biased analysis.

Transparent methodology requires explicit attention to source selection, interpretive frameworks, and potential biases that might influence analysis of religious violence. Scholars studying religious conflict must acknowledge their own religious or secular commitments, examine how these commitments might influence their interpretation of evidence, and develop strategies for testing their conclusions against alternative explanations. This methodological reflexivity becomes particularly important when studying contemporary conflicts where academic analysis might influence policy decisions or public opinion in ways that affect conflict dynamics. The goal involves developing analytical approaches that can identify patterns in religious violence without essentializing particular traditions or ignoring legitimate grievances that motivate religious mobilization.

Case study methodology provides one approach for developing transparent analysis of religious violence that avoids both relativistic abdication and biased interpretation. Comparative case studies can examine similar conflicts across different religious traditions to identify common patterns while respecting the specific theological, historical, and cultural contexts that shape particular conflicts. Process tracing methodologies can examine how religious and secular factors interact over time to produce violent outcomes while avoiding predetermined assumptions about religious or secular causation. Mixed-methods approaches can combine quantitative analysis of conflict patterns with qualitative examination of particular cases to test generalizations against detailed empirical evidence.

Religion and Armed Conflict dataset provides valuable resources for transparent analysis by systematically coding religious dimensions of contemporary conflicts while acknowledging the complexity of causal relationships. This dataset demonstrates that religious factors appear in approximately one-third of contemporary armed conflicts, but rarely as the sole cause of violence. Instead, religious elements typically interact with ethnic, territorial, and political factors in ways that intensify conflicts while making them more difficult to resolve through conventional diplomatic means. The quantitative evidence supports theoretical arguments about the multidimensional nature of religious conflict while providing empirical foundations for more detailed case study analysis.

Post-secular critiques of religious violence analysis challenge the secular-religious distinction that underlies much academic scholarship, arguing that this distinction reflects Western Protestant assumptions rather than universal analytical categories. Post-secular theorists contend that treating religion as a discrete domain separate from politics, economics, and culture reproduces colonial frameworks that misrepresent how most human societies organize meaning, authority, and social relationships. From this perspective, academic analysis of religious violence often reflects secular biases that privilege rational political explanations while treating religious motivations as irrational or pathological.

Jürgen Habermas's influential articulation of post-secular theory argues that contemporary societies must develop new frameworks for understanding the relationship between religious and secular worldviews that avoid both secular dismissal of religious insights and religious rejection of secular rationality. Habermas advocates "translation" processes that can bring religious ethical resources into public discourse while maintaining commitment to rational argumentation and inclusive deliberation. Applied to religious violence analysis, post-secular approaches would examine how religious and secular factors interpenetrate rather than treating them as distinct causal domains, while acknowledging both the insights and limitations that religious traditions offer for understanding and addressing violence.

However, engaging post-secular critiques does not require abandoning analytical distinctions between religious and secular factors or treating all explanatory frameworks as equally valid. The challenge involves developing more sophisticated approaches that can acknowledge the interpenetration of religious and secular dimensions while maintaining analytical clarity about causal relationships and policy implications. This requires recognizing that religious traditions contain both resources for peace and justifications for violence, that secular ideologies also legitimate both cooperation and conflict, and that the most dangerous forms of violence often emerge when religious absolutism combines with secular nationalism or political ideology.

Critics of post-secular approaches argue that they risk obscuring important differences between religious and secular forms of violence, potentially legitimizing religious extremism through false equivalencies with secular ideology. William Cavanaugh's argument that religious violence is a myth that serves Western secular interests faces criticism for downplaying genuine theological motivations for violence while overstating the peacefulness of secular political systems. Richard Dawkins and other critics contend that religious traditions' emphasis on faith, divine command, and ultimate truth creates distinctive psychological and social conditions that make religious violence qualitatively different from secular conflict.

Resolving these debates requires empirical examination of how religious and secular factors actually operate in particular conflicts rather than theoretical arguments about their essential characteristics. The evidence suggests that both religious and secular ideologies can motivate violence, that both provide resources for peaceful conflict resolution, and that the most intense conflicts often involve combinations of religious, ethnic, political, and economic factors that resist neat categorization. Rather than asking whether religion causes violence, more productive questions involve examining when religious factors become activated in conflicts, how religious and secular motivations interact, and what institutional arrangements can channel religious energy toward peaceful rather than violent ends.

Contemporary policy implications of religious violence analysis extend beyond academic debates to practical questions about conflict prevention, peacebuilding, and social cohesion in religiously diverse societies. Understanding the complex relationship between religious narrative and material factors provides crucial insights for developing effective interventions that address both the symbolic and structural dimensions of religious conflict. Successful peacebuilding initiatives typically combine efforts to promote interfaith dialogue and theological reflection with programs that address economic inequality, political exclusion, and institutional discrimination that provide grievances for religious mobilization.

The rise in global religious violence documented by organizations like the Pew Research Center requires sophisticated responses that avoid both security approaches that treat religious motivation as inherently pathological and multicultural approaches that avoid confronting extremist interpretations of religious traditions. Effective responses must work with religious communities to promote interpretations of their traditions that support peaceful coexistence while simultaneously addressing the social conditions—poverty, inequality, political exclusion, state failure—that make extremist religious narratives appealing to particular populations.

Faith-based peacebuilding initiatives demonstrate the potential for religious resources to contribute to conflict transformation rather than conflict escalation. Religious leaders possess distinctive authority within their communities, access to networks that cross conflict lines, and theological resources for promoting forgiveness, reconciliation, and nonviolent resistance that secular organizations often lack. However, these religious contributions to peacemaking require institutional support, protection from extremist threats, and integration with secular approaches that address structural causes of conflict.

The ultimate conclusion supports neither essentialist arguments that treat certain religions as inherently violent nor reductionist approaches that dismiss religious motivations as covers for material interests. Instead, religious violence emerges from complex interactions between theological narratives, social identity formation, material conditions, and institutional contexts that require sophisticated analysis acknowledging both religious and secular dimensions. Understanding these interactions provides essential foundation for developing policies that can promote religious freedom while preventing religious extremism, support faith-based peacebuilding while addressing structural injustices, and maintain analytical clarity about the sources of violence while respecting the legitimate spiritual needs that religious traditions serve for billions of people worldwide.

Chapter Ten
Primate Power Dynamics — The WIIFM Machine

Human social behavior reflects deep evolutionary inheritance from primate ancestors who survived through sophisticated alliance systems, status competitions, and resource acquisition strategies that continue operating beneath the veneer of modern civilization. Understanding these underlying dynamics requires examining what I term the "WIIFM machine"—the evolved psychological apparatus that constantly calculates "What's In It For Me" across social interactions, driving coalition formation, status seeking, and resource accumulation behaviors that religious institutions both exploit and attempt to channel. This analysis situates human behavior within broader evolutionary patterns while defending against charges of reductionism, biological determinism, or moral nihilism that such explanations often provoke. The primate power dynamics framework illuminates how religious systems function as sophisticated mechanisms for managing competitive impulses through transcendent narratives, moral frameworks, and institutional structures that redirect self-interested behavior toward collective goals. However, this evolutionary perspective must be defended against multiple objections: critics argue that emphasizing biological continuity reduces human complexity to animal behavior, that neurochemical explanations ignore cultural sophistication, and that transactional models cynically dismiss genuine altruism and spiritual experience. Additionally, the framework faces challenges from those who contend that evolutionary explanations provide post-hoc justifications for existing inequalities rather than scientifically grounded analyses of human nature.

Coalition formation among primates represents one of evolution's most sophisticated strategies for navigating competitive social environments, providing crucial insights into human political, economic, and religious alliances that contemporary societies often misunderstand or romanticize. Primate coalitions emerge when individuals calculate that cooperative action will yield better outcomes than solitary competition, creating temporary or permanent alliances that can dramatically alter dominance hierarchies, resource access, and reproductive opportunities. These coalitions operate according to principles that evolutionary biologists characterize as "banana grabs"—strategic alliances aimed at securing valuable resources, whether food, territory, mates, or social position. The mathematical models developed by researchers like Pandit and van Schaik reveal that coalition formation follows predictable patterns based on individual strength rankings, potential benefits of cooperation, and costs of conflict, with successful coalitions requiring both profitability (all participants gain net benefits) and feasibility (the coalition possesses sufficient strength to achieve its objectives).

However, the complexity of primate coalition behavior extends far beyond simple resource acquisition, involving sophisticated social calculations about trust, reciprocity, future interactions, and reputation management that challenge reductionist interpretations. Recent research demonstrates that bonobos and chimpanzees exhibit different coalition strategies: chimpanzees more frequently form conservative coalitions (dominant individuals attacking lower-ranking targets) and engage in coordinated group aggression, while bonobos more often pursue individual aggressive encounters without coalitionary support. These differences reflect distinct evolutionary adaptations to varying ecological pressures, social structures, and resource distribution patterns rather than representing fixed behavioral templates. The neurobiological analysis reveals that bonobos possess enhanced neural circuitry for perceiving distress in others and superior pathways linking the amygdala with ventral anterior cingulate cortex, supporting increased empathic sensitivity and better top-down control of aggressive impulses compared to chimpanzees.

Defending the coalitional analysis against charges of crude reductionism requires situating these behavioral patterns within evolutionary theory responsibly, acknowledging both the sophisticated cognitive processes involved in alliance formation and the cultural innovations that distinguish human coalition behavior from other primates. Human coalitions operate through symbolic communication, abstract reasoning about future scenarios, moral frameworks that justify cooperative action, and institutional structures that extend beyond immediate kinship or territorial groups. Religious coalitions exemplify this complexity by combining evolutionary motivations (group solidarity, resource pooling, status competition) with transcendent narratives that provide meaning beyond material advantage.

RELIGION AS A MIND PAINTING

The Catholic Church, Islamic ummah, Buddhist sangha, and other religious coalitions create imagined communities that span continents and centuries, enabling cooperation among genetically unrelated individuals through shared beliefs, ritual practices, and moral commitments that exceed the scope of primate alliance systems while building upon their underlying psychological foundations.

The neurochemical reward systems underlying status seeking provide essential insights into why humans invest enormous energy in acquiring and maintaining social rank, often through religious participation that offers prestige, authority, and recognition within particular communities. Dopamine pathways in the mesolimbic and mesocortical systems evolved to reinforce behaviors that enhanced reproductive success in ancestral environments, including successful competition for dominance positions that provided preferential access to mates, resources, and social support. Contemporary neuroscientific research demonstrates that social status achievements activate the same reward circuits that respond to food, sex, and addictive substances, explaining why status competition can become compulsive and why individuals often sacrifice material wellbeing to maintain social position. The dopaminergic response to status elevation operates through prediction error signaling—when individuals achieve higher rank than expected, dopamine neurons fire more intensely, creating powerful reinforcement for status-seeking behaviors.

Religious institutions exploit these neurochemical systems by providing multiple pathways for status acquisition: theological expertise, moral authority, ritual leadership, charitable contributions, missionary activity, and mystical experience all offer opportunities for recognition and rank advancement within religious communities. The Catholic priesthood, Islamic scholarship, Buddhist monasticism, and Protestant pastoral authority create elaborate hierarchies that channel competitive impulses toward spiritual goals while providing neurochemical rewards for successful advancement. However, these systems also generate problematic dynamics when status competition overwhelms spiritual purposes, leading to corruption, authoritarianism, and exploitation that religious traditions themselves often condemn. The scandals plaguing various religious institutions—financial corruption, sexual abuse, political manipulation—frequently reflect unregulated status competition that religious frameworks prove insufficient to control.

Defending against charges of overemphasizing neurochemical factors requires acknowledging that biological reward systems provide necessary but not sufficient explanations for human behavior, operating within cultural contexts that shape how status is defined, acquired, and expressed. Human status systems exhibit remarkable cultural variation: some societies emphasize warrior prowess, others scholarly achievement, still others spiritual purity or artistic creativity. Religious traditions typically attempt to redirect status competition away from material accumulation or physical dominance toward moral development, spiritual insight, and service to transcendent purposes. The Buddhist emphasis on ego dissolution, Christian ideals of humility and self-sacrifice, and Islamic concepts of submission to Allah represent sophisticated attempts to transcend rather than simply redirect competitive impulses, even when these ideals remain imperfectly realized in practice.

The Iron Law of Oligarchy, formulated by Robert Michels through his analysis of early 20th-century socialist parties, provides crucial insights into how democratic movements and religious organizations inevitably develop elite leadership structures that concentrate power despite egalitarian founding principles. Michels observed that organizational effectiveness requires specialized knowledge, centralized coordination, and professional leadership that create conditions where small groups of leaders acquire disproportionate influence over larger memberships. As organizations grow larger and more complex, the technical demands of administration, communication, and strategic planning necessitate bureaucratic structures that create opportunities for oligarchical control, even within movements explicitly committed to democratic participation and egalitarian principles.

Religious institutions exemplify oligarchical tendencies through their development of clerical hierarchies, doctrinal authorities, and administrative bureaucracies that concentrate interpretive and executive power in elite groups despite theological commitments to spiritual equality. The Catholic Church's papal authority and episcopal hierarchy, Protestant denominational structures with professional clergy, Islamic scholarly establishments, and Buddhist monastic hierarchies all demonstrate how religious movements that begin with egalitarian impulses develop oligarchical characteristics as they institutionalize. The early Christian community's emphasis on the priesthood of all believers gradually gave way to episcopal authority and papal supremacy; Islamic ideals of consultation (shura) and community consensus (ijma) became dominated by scholarly elites and political authorities; Buddhist emphasis on individual enlightenment developed into monastic institutions with elaborate rank systems and hierarchical controls.

However, discussing exceptions and limitations to the Iron Law requires acknowledging both successful examples of democratic religious governance and ongoing tensions between oligarchical tendencies and egalitarian impulses within religious institutions. The Religious Society of Friends (Quakers) has maintained relatively egalitarian decision-making processes through business meetings that seek spiritual consensus rather than hierarchical authority, though these practices work primarily in small-scale communities with shared cultural backgrounds. Congregational Protestant denominations preserve significant local autonomy and democratic governance, though they often develop informal leadership oligarchies. Contemporary liberation theology movements, feminist theology, and indigenous religious revitalization demonstrate ongoing efforts to democratize religious authority and challenge oligarchical control, with varying degrees of success depending on institutional contexts and external pressures.

The theoretical framework must acknowledge that oligarchical tendencies represent organizational dynamics rather than inevitable laws, creating ongoing tensions between democratic aspirations and hierarchical necessities that different religious traditions navigate through various institutional innovations. Michels himself recognized that the Iron Law describes one tendency within organizations rather than deterministic outcomes, noting that democratic ideals continue providing resources for challenging oligarchical consolidation through reform movements, leadership changes, and institutional restructuring. Religious institutions demonstrate this dynamism through periodic revival movements, reformist initiatives, and prophetic challenges to established authority that can temporarily or permanently alter power relationships within religious communities.

The WIIFM machine represents the evolved psychological apparatus that constantly evaluates social interactions through cost-benefit calculations aimed at maximizing individual advantage while managing competitive pressures through cooperative strategies. Transactional Analysis, developed by Eric Berne, provides valuable insights into how these calculations operate through Parent, Adult, and Child ego states that shape interpersonal communications and relationship dynamics. The Parent ego state incorporates internalized authority figures and moral frameworks, the Adult ego state engages in rational problem-solving and information processing, while the Child ego state expresses emotional needs, creative impulses, and adaptive responses to social pressures. Religious participation involves complex transactions among these ego states: individuals may seek parental authority through religious teaching, adult understanding through theological study, and child-like wonder through spiritual experience, while simultaneously offering their own resources and commitments in exchange for community belonging, moral guidance, and transcendent meaning.

The transactional calculus underlying religious participation operates through multiple exchange relationships: time and energy for social connection, financial contributions for institutional services, moral conformity for community acceptance, and spiritual devotion for promised salvation or enlightenment. These transactions often remain unconscious or become rationalized through theological frameworks that emphasize altruistic motivations while masking underlying self-interested calculations. However, distinguishing the descriptive model from normative endorsement is crucial for maintaining analytical objectivity while avoiding cynical dismissal of genuine spiritual motivations. The fact that religious behavior serves individual interests does not invalidate its spiritual significance or moral value, any more than recognizing that parental love has evolutionary functions diminishes its emotional authenticity.

Religious institutions successfully channel transactional motivations by providing frameworks that align individual self-interest with collective welfare and transcendent purposes. The Christian concept of mutual edification suggests that serving others ultimately benefits oneself through spiritual growth and community strengthening. Islamic principles of giving (zakat) and pilgrimage (hajj) create systems where individual religious obligations contribute to collective welfare and spiritual development. Buddhist teachings about interdependence and compassion frame individual liberation as inseparable from universal compassion, making personal spiritual progress dependent on concern for all sentient beings. These theological frameworks transform apparently selfish motivations into vehicles for genuine spiritual development and moral growth, though they remain vulnerable to manipulation when transactional calculations overwhelm transcendent commitments.

The principle of "Finders Keepers, Losers Weepers" reflects deep evolutionary inheritance regarding resource acquisition and territorial control that continues shaping contemporary economic, political, and religious competition despite moral frameworks that challenge these impulses. Primate studies reveal that successful resource acquisition depends on combination of individual strength, social alliances, and strategic positioning that enable groups to secure and defend valuable resources against competitors. Human societies have developed elaborate legal and ethical systems aimed at regulating resource competition through property rights, distributive justice, and moral obligations that transcend mere possession, but these cultural innovations often conflict with underlying psychological tendencies toward resource maximization and group favoritism.

Religious traditions typically challenge "Finders Keepers" mentality through teachings about stewardship, sharing, and transcendent values that subordinate material accumulation to spiritual development. Christian teachings about the dangers of wealth, Islamic principles of economic justice, Buddhist warnings about attachment to material possessions, and indigenous traditions emphasizing reciprocity and gift-giving all provide alternatives to purely competitive resource acquisition. However, these religious ideals often coexist uneasily with practical necessities of institutional maintenance, individual survival, and group competition that make complete abandonment of acquisitive behavior unrealistic. Contemporary prosperity theology, religious nationalism, and institutional wealth accumulation demonstrate how religious frameworks can be co-opted to justify rather than challenge competitive resource acquisition.

Incorporating legal and ethical critiques requires acknowledging both the evolutionary persistence of competitive impulses and the cultural innovations that enable transcendence of purely self-interested behavior. Modern legal systems attempt to balance individual property rights with collective welfare through taxation, regulation, and redistribution mechanisms that reflect ongoing negotiations between acquisitive impulses and moral obligations. Religious traditions contribute to these negotiations by providing transcendent frameworks that motivate voluntary sharing, ethical business practices, and concern for marginalized populations who lack resources to compete effectively in market systems. The most successful approaches combine realistic acknowledgment of competitive human nature with institutional structures that channel these impulses toward socially beneficial outcomes while providing spiritual resources for individual transformation.

Propaganda and narrative manipulation represent sophisticated mechanisms through which religious and political leaders shape public perception, manage dissent, and maintain authority by controlling information flows and interpretive frameworks. The psychological mechanisms underlying propaganda effectiveness exploit evolved cognitive biases toward in-group loyalty, authority deference, and emotional rather than rational decision-making that religious institutions both utilize and claim to transcend. Effective propaganda operates through repetitive messaging that desensitizes critical faculties, emotional appeals that bypass rational evaluation, and narrative frameworks that provide simple explanations for complex phenomena while identifying clear enemies and allies. Religious propaganda employs sacred texts, authoritative interpretations, ritual reinforcement, and community pressure to maintain doctrinal orthodoxy while suppressing contradictory evidence or alternative explanations.

However, acknowledging the complexity of ideological critique requires recognizing that not all religious messaging constitutes manipulation, and that distinguishing between legitimate spiritual teaching and propagandistic control involves difficult judgments about intentions, effects, and institutional contexts. Religious traditions claim to provide authentic spiritual guidance based on divine revelation, accumulated wisdom, and contemplative insight that transcends merely human knowledge, making simple categorization as propaganda inappropriate. The challenge involves developing analytical frameworks that can identify manipulative uses of religious authority while respecting legitimate spiritual teaching and community formation. This requires examining whether religious messaging promotes critical thinking or discourages questioning, whether it encourages engagement with alternative perspectives or demands exclusive loyalty, and whether it serves primarily institutional interests or genuine human flourishing.

Contemporary digital environments create unprecedented opportunities for propaganda and narrative manipulation through targeted messaging, algorithm-driven content delivery, and social media echo chambers that amplify confirming information while filtering out contradictory perspectives. Religious communities navigate these environments with varying degrees of sophistication, sometimes utilizing digital tools effectively for genuine spiritual formation and community building while other times falling victim to manipulative messaging or contributing to information pollution through uncritical promotion of partisan political positions disguised as religious teaching. The most constructive approaches involve media literacy education, transparent communication practices, and institutional commitments to intellectual honesty that model the values they claim to represent.

Bonobo cooperation provides important correctives to oversimplified narratives about human nature that emphasize only competitive and aggressive dimensions of primate inheritance. Recent research challenges popular characterizations of bonobos as uniformly peaceful, revealing that male bonobos actually engage in aggressive behavior more frequently than chimpanzees, but their aggression follows different patterns: bonobos target almost exclusively other males rather than females, rarely form coalitions for coordinated attacks, and never engage in lethal violence against conspecifics. These differences reflect distinct evolutionary adaptations rather than moral superiority, with bonobo societies characterized by female dominance, frequent sexual behavior that diffuses tension, and intergroup interactions that can be either hostile or affiliative depending on circumstances.

The neurobiological differences between bonobos and chimpanzees provide insights into the neural mechanisms underlying cooperative versus competitive behavior that apply to human social organization. Bonobos possess enhanced brain regions involved in perceiving distress in others, larger pathways connecting emotional centers with cognitive control areas, and neurochemical systems that support empathic sensitivity and tension reduction through affiliative behavior. However, avoiding simplistic moral dichotomies requires acknowledging that both cooperative and competitive strategies serve important functions in different ecological and social contexts, and that human societies require institutional frameworks capable of channeling both impulses toward constructive outcomes rather than simply celebrating one tendency while condemning the other.

Religious traditions demonstrate sophisticated understanding of the need to balance cooperative and competitive impulses through institutional structures that promote both individual excellence and collective welfare. Monastic communities create environments that support contemplative development while requiring cooperative participation in community life. Religious education systems encourage intellectual achievement and spiritual advancement while emphasizing service to others and institutional loyalty. Missionary activities combine competitive elements (evangelistic success, church growth) with cooperative goals (cultural bridge-building, humanitarian service). The most successful religious institutions develop cultures that channel competitive energy toward spiritually productive goals while maintaining communal solidarity and mutual support.

The integration of evolutionary psychology, neuroscience, and social analysis reveals human behavior as emerging from complex interactions between inherited psychological mechanisms, cultural learning, and institutional structures that resist simple reduction to either biological or cultural determinism. The WIIFM machine operates through sophisticated cognitive and emotional systems that evolved to navigate competitive social environments through strategic cooperation, status acquisition, and resource maximization, but these systems operate within cultural contexts that profoundly shape their expression and provide opportunities for transcendence through moral development and spiritual practice. Religious institutions represent humanity's most ambitious attempts to channel competitive impulses toward transcendent purposes while providing meaning, community, and moral guidance that serve genuine human needs even when they also exploit underlying psychological mechanisms for institutional advantage.

Understanding these dynamics provides essential insights for developing more effective approaches to religious education, institutional reform, and spiritual practice that can acknowledge human psychological realities while promoting authentic development toward compassion, wisdom, and service to the common good. The goal involves neither naive dismissal of competitive human nature nor cynical reduction of spiritual aspirations to mere biological programming, but rather sophisticated integration of scientific understanding with moral vision that can guide individual and collective transformation. This requires ongoing dialogue between evolutionary insights and religious wisdom that honors both scientific accuracy and spiritual authenticity while remaining committed to human flourishing in all its dimensions.

Chapter Eleven
Religion as Cultural Heritage

Religious traditions function not merely as systems of belief and practice but as dynamic repositories of cultural heritage that preserve, transmit, and continuously reinterpret collective memory, artistic expression, moral frameworks, and communal identity across generations. The concept of "culturalized religion" highlights how religious communities serve as active agents in heritage processes rather than passive objects of preservation managed by secular institutions. This framework challenges traditional heritage studies approaches that often separate cultural value from spiritual significance, revealing instead how religious meaning and cultural transmission remain deeply interconnected. Contemporary scholarship must engage with heritage studies critiques of authenticity, commodification, and power dynamics while examining the increasingly fluid boundaries between secular and religious domains in hybrid cultural practices. Simultaneously, the global resurgence of religion amid widespread cultural drift demands explanation that avoids teleological assumptions about inevitable returns to tradition while accounting for religion's remarkable adaptive capacity and institutional resilience.

The emergence of culturalized religion as an analytical framework reflects growing recognition that religious traditions serve multiple functions simultaneously: spiritual guidance for believers, cultural identity markers for communities, and heritage resources for broader societies. UNESCO's Initiative on Heritage of Religious Interest acknowledges that approximately twenty percent of World Heritage Sites possess religious or spiritual connections, requiring management approaches that balance conservation objectives with ongoing religious practice. The 2003 Convention for the Safeguarding of Intangible Cultural Heritage further recognizes religious rituals, oral traditions, and ceremonial practices as forms of living heritage that require community-led preservation strategies rather than museum-style conservation. These policy developments reflect theoretical shifts in heritage studies that foreground practitioner agency and cultural rights over expert-driven preservation models that historically marginalized religious communities from decisions about their own traditions.

However, engaging heritage studies critiques requires acknowledging how state institutions, international organizations, and heritage professionals often appropriate religious sites and practices for purposes that serve tourism revenue, national branding, or secular educational objectives while potentially undermining the spiritual needs and cultural autonomy of religious practitioners. The inscription of Varanasi's ghats on the World Heritage List celebrates their millennia-old ritual significance but primarily benefits heritage tourism infrastructure and municipal authorities while requiring local priests and pilgrims to navigate regulatory frameworks that restrict traditional offering practices and ritual access. Similarly, Jerusalem's Old City designation as World Heritage recognizes its significance for Judaism, Christianity, and Islam but operates through international governance mechanisms that often prioritize archaeological preservation over the daily religious life of communities whose living traditions constitute the city's spiritual significance.

The Palestinian Territories' nomination of the Church of the Nativity and the Pilgrimage Route in Bethlehem illustrates how religious heritage becomes entangled with contested sovereignty and political identity formation. Palestinian authorities used UNESCO inscription processes to assert cultural and political claims over territories under Israeli occupation, while Israeli authorities argued that Palestinian heritage management capabilities remained inadequate to protect Christian sacred sites. The resulting inscription in 2012 represented both recognition of Palestinian cultural rights and a diplomatic victory that enhanced Palestinian claims to statehood, demonstrating how religious heritage functions as a resource in broader struggles over political recognition and territorial control.

Participatory heritage governance models offer promising alternatives that foreground religious communities as primary stakeholders in heritage processes while respecting both cultural rights and conservation objectives. Indigenous Australian collaborations with heritage agencies to document Dreamtime ceremony sites illustrate how community-led heritage planning can integrate traditional knowledge systems with contemporary preservation technologies. Aboriginal elders retain decision-making authority over which aspects of sacred geography become public heritage resources while using digital mapping and video documentation to ensure cultural transmission to younger generations. Similarly, Yoruba communities in Nigeria collaborate with ethnomusicologists to create digital archives of Ifá divination chants that preserve sacred oral traditions while maintaining community control over access protocols and ritual usage.

Japanese Shinto shrine associations demonstrate another model of participatory heritage governance through collaborative mapping projects that document shrine precincts, festival traditions, and ritual landscapes. Local parishioners (ujiko) work with heritage professionals to create comprehensive inventories of material culture—torii gates, ritual implements, architectural details—alongside intangible practices like seasonal festivals, purification ceremonies, and community governance traditions. These projects enable shrine communities to access heritage funding for building maintenance and festival support while ensuring that heritage designation enhances rather than constrains ongoing religious practice. The success of such collaborative approaches depends on institutional frameworks that recognize religious communities' intellectual property rights over their traditions while providing technical and financial resources for heritage preservation activities.

The fluidity of boundaries between secular and religious domains emerges clearly in hybrid cultural phenomena where religious and secular identities intersect through festivals, consumer practices, civic ceremonies, and individual self-fashioning. European "cultural Catholics" exemplify this boundary fluidity by participating in religious festivals like Spain's Semana Santa processions or Italy's patron saint celebrations as expressions of regional identity and cultural heritage rather than theological commitment. These participants often describe their involvement in terms of cultural belonging, aesthetic appreciation, and community solidarity while maintaining agnostic or secular worldviews regarding Catholic doctrinal teachings. Such hybrid participation challenges analytical frameworks that treat religious involvement as necessarily requiring belief commitments, revealing instead how religious practices can function as cultural heritage resources for broader community identity formation.

The phenomenon of "spiritual but not religious" (SBNR) identities in North America illustrates another dimension of secular-religious boundary fluidity through the appropriation of religious practices within secular therapeutic and wellness frameworks. SBNR practitioners commonly engage in Buddhist mindfulness meditation, Hindu yoga practices, and New Age ritual adaptations while explicitly rejecting institutional religious affiliation and doctrinal orthodoxy. This selective appropriation transforms religious practices into lifestyle choices and personal development technologies that operate within consumer markets rather than traditional religious authority structures. Critics argue that such appropriation represents cultural colonialism that extracts spiritual techniques from their cultural contexts while ignoring their theological foundations, but proponents emphasize individual autonomy and spiritual exploration as legitimate forms of religious engagement.

Japanese New Year shrine visits (hatsumode) provide another example of boundary fluidity where nominally secular populations engage in religious practices as cultural tradition rather than theological commitment. Surveys indicate that many hatsumode participants report no personal belief in Shinto deities while still finding meaning in ritual purification, prayer offerings, and festival participation as expressions of Japanese cultural identity and community belonging. The Japanese case illustrates how secularization processes can coexist with ongoing religious practice when religious activities become reinterpreted as cultural heritage practices that reinforce national or regional identity rather than supernatural belief systems.

Brazil's Afro-Brazilian religious traditions demonstrate more complex forms of boundary fluidity where Candomblé terreiros serve simultaneously as religious communities for initiates and cultural heritage sites for broader Brazilian identity formation. Candomblé public festivals (festas) attract participants who range from committed practitioners seeking spiritual guidance to secular participants celebrating Afro-Brazilian culture as resistance to European colonial heritage. State cultural agencies now provide funding support for Candomblé festivals as expressions of Brazilian multicultural heritage while terreiro leaders navigate tensions between maintaining ritual authenticity for religious purposes and adapting ceremonies for public consumption. The success of these negotiations demonstrates how religious communities can leverage heritage frameworks to gain social recognition and resource access while preserving essential spiritual functions.

Defending against boundary theory critiques requires acknowledging both the analytical utility of distinguishing secular and religious orientations for understanding different motivations and meanings while recognizing the empirical reality of their porous boundaries in lived experience. American presidential inaugurations exemplify institutional boundary fluidity through ceremonies that combine secular constitutional procedures with religious invocations, chaplain services, and biblical references that reflect the nation's religious heritage while attempting to maintain constitutional church-state separation. Turkey's Hagia Sophia provides another example of institutional boundary negotiation through its successive functions as Byzantine cathedral, Ottoman Mosque, secular museum, and restored mosque, with each transition reflecting different approaches to managing religious and secular claims on the same architectural heritage.

Contemporary research on religious "nones" reveals significant internal diversity within populations that claim no religious preference, including substantial numbers who maintain spiritual beliefs, engage in religious practices, or identify with religious cultural heritage despite rejecting institutional affiliation. Survey research indicates that religious nones include both secular individuals who reject all supernatural beliefs and "liminal" individuals who maintain ambiguous relationships with religious traditions through selective practice, cultural identification, or spiritual exploration without institutional commitment. This internal diversity challenges assumptions about secularization as necessarily involving complete abandonment of religious culture, revealing instead how individuals can maintain complex, situational relationships with religious heritage that resist simple secular-religious categorizations.

Religion's global resurgence amid cultural drift challenges classic secularization theories that predicted religion's inevitable decline with modernization, industrialization, and scientific advancement. Instead of uniform secularization, empirical evidence reveals varied trajectories across different regions and religious traditions: Pentecostal growth in sub-Saharan Africa and Latin America, Islamic revival movements across Muslim-majority societies, Hindu nationalism's expansion in India, Orthodox Christianity's revival in Eastern Europe, and indigenous religious movements throughout the Global South. These patterns reflect religion's adaptive capacity to address social needs, provide collective identity, and offer meaning-making resources during periods of rapid social change, economic disruption, and cultural uncertainty rather than representing predetermined returns to pre-modern traditionalism.

Pentecostal Christianity's rapid expansion across the Global South illustrates how religious movements succeed by filling social niches created by state institutional weakness, economic inequality, and cultural dislocation. Pentecostal churches provide healthcare services, educational opportunities, microfinance programs, and social support networks that supplement inadequate government services while offering spiritual resources for coping with poverty, illness, and social marginalization. The Pentecostal emphasis on prosperity theology, divine healing, and individual empowerment appeals particularly to populations experiencing economic precarity and social exclusion, providing both practical assistance and transcendent hope for material improvement. Research indicates that Pentecostal growth correlates with urbanization, economic liberalization, and state capacity limitations rather than representing resistance to modernity per se.

China's state-sponsored revival of Confucian rituals and cultural traditions demonstrates how governments can leverage religious heritage for political legitimacy and social cohesion during periods of rapid economic transformation. The Chinese Communist Party's promotion of Confucian values through educational curricula, public ceremonies, and international Confucius Institutes represents strategic deployment of traditional cultural resources to address social problems created by market reforms: increasing inequality, environmental degradation, corruption, and social fragmentation. This instrumentalization of religious heritage for state purposes illustrates how secularization and religious revival can occur simultaneously when governments appropriate religious cultural resources for governance objectives while maintaining ideological commitment to secular political authority.

Hindu nationalist movements in India exemplify how religious resurgence becomes entangled with cultural identity politics, territorial claims, and resistance to globalization pressures. The Bharatiya Janata Party's promotion of Hindutva ideology links Hindu religious identity with Indian national identity through temple construction campaigns, festival celebrations, and heritage preservation projects that assert Hindu cultural dominance over religious minorities. These movements combine religious symbolism with political mobilization around issues like temple restoration, cow protection, and opposition to Islamic architecture that appeal to Hindu cultural pride while advancing partisan political objectives. The success of Hindu nationalism reflects anxieties about cultural authenticity, demographic change, and foreign influence that religious identity provides resources for addressing even when political rather than theological concerns drive mobilization.

Liberation Theology in Latin America demonstrates how religious traditions can generate counter-hegemonic movements that challenge existing power structures through theological reinterpretation and grassroots organizing. Catholic base communities throughout Brazil, El Salvador, and Nicaragua during the 1970s-1990s used biblical exegesis to justify land reform, labor rights, and political resistance to military regimes and economic exploitation. Liberation theologians leveraged traditional Catholic authority while developing theological innovations—preferential option for the poor, structural sin analysis, praxis-based methodology—that supported social justice activism and democratic political participation. The movement's decline following Vatican pressure and democratic transitions illustrates how religious resurgence depends on specific political contexts and institutional support systems rather than representing inevitable religious vitality.

Explaining religious resilience without teleological assumptions requires attention to ecological niche theory and institutional adaptation rather than claims about essential religious needs or inevitable spiritual awakenings. Religious institutions succeed when they exploit social niches created by rapid social change: providing community solidarity during urbanization, moral guidance during cultural transitions, social services during state capacity limitations, and identity resources during globalization pressures. Successful religious movements demonstrate remarkable adaptive capacity through theological innovation, organizational flexibility, and cultural translation that enables them to address contemporary needs while maintaining continuity with traditional resources. However, this adaptive success depends on favorable social conditions rather than representing predetermined religious revival or teleological return to traditional values.

Post-secular theoretical frameworks developed by scholars like José Casanova and Peter Berger provide essential tools for understanding religion's continued public relevance without assuming either inevitable secularization or religious resurgence. Casanova's concept of "deprivatization" describes how religious traditions have reentered public spheres through social movements, political activism, and civil society organizations that challenge earlier assumptions about religion's privatization in modern societies. His analysis of "multiple modernities" acknowledges diverse pathways of social development where secularization and religious vitality can coexist rather than representing mutually exclusive alternatives. Berger's later reflections on post-secularism emphasize religious and secular worldview's ongoing interaction in pluralistic societies where neither achieves complete cultural hegemony.

Contemporary empirical research supports post-secular insights through documentation of religious organizations' extensive roles in global governance, social welfare, and cultural preservation that transcend simple belief-based categorizations. Religious NGOs provide significant portions of healthcare, education, and humanitarian assistance worldwide through organizations like Catholic Relief Services, Islamic Relief Worldwide, and Buddhist Tzu Chi Foundation that operate alongside secular development agencies. Interfaith initiatives address climate change, peacebuilding, and human rights through collaborative projects that leverage religious communities' moral authority and organizational capacity while engaging secular policy frameworks. Religious heritage tourism generates substantial economic activity while supporting cultural preservation and community development in both developed and developing societies.

The political economy of religious heritage requires critical examination of how tourism commodification, intellectual property appropriation, and market-driven development affect religious communities and cultural authenticity. Heritage tourism at religious sites generates billions of dollars annually through pilgrim accommodation, ritual participation fees, and souvenir sales that can provide crucial income for local communities while potentially undermining spiritual atmospheres and traditional practices. The commercialization of yoga practices through corporate wellness programs, the patenting of indigenous healing techniques, and the trademarking of religious symbols illustrate how market forces can extract cultural resources from religious communities while providing minimal compensation or recognition for traditional knowledge holders.

UNESCO World Heritage designation often increases tourism pressure on religious sites while providing limited resources for managing visitor impacts on ongoing religious practice. Machu Picchu's designation as both World Heritage Site and Indigenous sacred landscape creates ongoing tensions between tourism development and Quechua community spiritual practices, while Angkor Wat's status as Cambodia's premier tourist destination affects Buddhist monastic communities whose traditional relationship with the temple complex becomes subordinated to heritage management priorities. Successful heritage management requires balancing economic benefits with cultural sustainability through community-controlled tourism initiatives, benefit-sharing agreements, and visitor education programs that respect religious sensitivities while supporting local development needs.

Ethical frameworks for religious heritage governance must address power imbalances between heritage professionals and religious communities while ensuring that cultural preservation serves community needs rather than external interests. Community-controlled heritage initiatives like Indigenous intellectual property protocols, traditional knowledge licensing systems, and heritage impact assessments provide models for protecting religious communities' cultural rights while enabling sustainable development and cross-cultural exchange. Fair trade religious artisan cooperatives, community-managed pilgrimage tourism, and heritage-based education programs demonstrate approaches that distribute economic benefits equitably while maintaining cultural authenticity and spiritual integrity.

Digital technologies create new opportunities and challenges for religious heritage preservation through virtual reality pilgrimage experiences, online ritual participation platforms, and digital archives of sacred texts and oral traditions. The COVID-19 pandemic accelerated religious communities' adoption of digital platforms for worship, education, and community formation while raising questions about the relationship between virtual and physical religious experience. Three-dimensional documentation of heritage sites like Palmyra's destroyed temples enables virtual reconstruction and educational access while providing limited substitutes for embodied religious practice and community gathering. Community-controlled digital platforms can support heritage transmission and diaspora connection while requiring careful attention to data sovereignty, cultural protocols, and technological equity issues.

Methodologically, comprehensive analysis of religion as cultural heritage requires multi-scalar research designs that integrate macro-level policy analysis with meso-level institutional ethnography and micro-level practice documentation. Ethnographic fieldwork provides essential insights into how religious communities experience heritage processes, navigate institutional pressures, and maintain cultural authenticity while engaging global heritage frameworks. Archival research illuminates historical patterns of religious-state relationships, heritage policy development, and community responses to external preservation initiatives. Digital humanities projects enable collaborative documentation and community-controlled heritage creation while requiring ongoing attention to ethical protocols and community consent processes.

The ultimate conclusion recognizes religion as cultural heritage as involving dynamic negotiations between tradition and innovation, community autonomy and external recognition, spiritual authenticity and cultural sustainability that resist simple preservation or commodification models. Culturalized religion frameworks foreground religious communities' agency in defining and managing their heritage while acknowledging the complex power dynamics that shape heritage processes in globalized contexts. Boundary fluidity analysis reveals how secular and religious orientations interact in hybrid practices that challenge rigid analytical categories while maintaining distinctive functions and meanings. Resilience studies explain religious adaptation and resurgence through ecological and institutional factors rather than teleological assumptions about spiritual inevitability. Post-secular perspectives provide theoretical resources for understanding religion's ongoing public relevance while avoiding both secularist dismissal and religious triumphalism. This integrated approach enables scholars and practitioners to support authentic heritage transmission while respecting cultural rights, promoting sustainable development, and fostering intercultural understanding in an increasingly connected yet diverse world

Chapter Twelve
Phenomenology of Meaning

Religious experience unfolds in dimensions that resist easy translation into the language of scientific explanation or sociological analysis. When a devout Muslim performs the dawn prayer (fajr), when a Catholic contemplative enters into silent adoration before the Blessed Sacrament, when a Hindu devotee experiences darshan at a temple, or when a Zen practitioner sits in zazen meditation, something occurs that exceeds behavioral description or neurological measurement. These moments constitute what phenomenologists call "lived experience"—consciousness engaged with phenomena as they appear, saturated with meaning that emerges through the dynamic interaction between perceiving subject and appearing world. Phenomenological inquiry takes this experiential dimension seriously, seeking to understand religious life on its own terms rather than reducing it to causal explanations derived from neuroscience, evolutionary psychology, or social theory.

The phenomenological approach, pioneered by Edmund Husserl and developed through the work of Martin Heidegger, Maurice Merleau-Ponty, and contemporary scholars in religious studies, offers rigorous methods for describing the structures of religious experience while avoiding both naive subjectivism and reductive scientism. However, this methodology faces persistent criticism from multiple directions: empirical scientists argue that phenomenology lacks objective validation; critical theorists contend that it ignores power dynamics and social construction; and analytic philosophers question whether subjective reports can yield reliable knowledge about religious phenomena. This chapter engages these critiques while demonstrating how phenomenological analysis provides essential insights into the meaning-making processes that constitute religious life, the relationship between habitual and reflective religious practice, and the methodological frameworks needed for rigorous investigation of religious experience that respects both scientific standards and spiritual authenticity.

Understanding religious experience on its own terms requires what Husserl called the "phenomenological epoché"—a methodological suspension of assumptions about the objective reality of religious phenomena in order to focus on how these phenomena appear in consciousness. This epoché does not deny the possible objective existence of divine realities but brackets ontological questions to attend to the structures of intentionality through which religious meaning emerges. When a Christian mystic reports experiencing divine presence during contemplative prayer, phenomenological analysis does not adjudicate the metaphysical truth of this experience but examines how divine presence appears: its temporal structure (eternal now versus sequential duration), spatial characteristics (omnipresent intimacy versus localized encounter), affective tonality (overwhelming love, peaceful union, fearful awe), and transformative effects (moral purification, enhanced compassion, deepened humility).

This approach reveals that religious experience involves complex intentional structures where consciousness is always consciousness-of-something, and that something in religious contexts carries distinctive phenomenological signatures. The "noetic-noematic correlation"—the relationship between the conscious act (noesis) and its intentional object (noema)—in religious experience typically involves what Jean-Luc Marion calls "saturated phenomena" that overflow conceptual containment and challenge ordinary modes of representation. A pilgrim's experience of the sacred at Lourdes or Varanasi cannot be adequately captured through photographs, theological propositions, or psychological explanations because the phenomenon saturates consciousness with meaning that exceeds available conceptual frameworks while simultaneously calling forth responses—reverence, gratitude, surrender—that constitute the religious subject's deepened participation in sacred reality.

Defending against reductionist critiques requires distinguishing between phenomenological description and causal explanation while demonstrating their complementary rather than competitive relationship. Neuroscientific research on religious experience—such as studies documenting changes in brain activity during prayer, meditation, or religious ecstasy—provides valuable data about the neurological correlates of religious states without necessarily explaining away the meaning and significance that these experiences hold for practitioners. The fact that mystical visions involve altered activity in visual cortex regions, that contemplative prayer correlates with decreased default mode network activation, or that religious conversion experiences show distinctive patterns of prefrontal and limbic engagement does not invalidate the spiritual significance these experiences hold within religious frameworks of meaning.

Contemporary neurophenomenology offers promising approaches for integrating first-person experiential reports with third-person neurological data through collaborative research methods that treat contemplative practitioners as expert investigators of consciousness rather than passive research subjects. Studies involving advanced meditators from Tibetan Buddhist, Christian contemplative, and Islamic Sufi traditions demonstrate how detailed phenomenological descriptions of contemplative states can inform experimental design and interpretation of neuroimaging data while the neurological findings illuminate aspects of contemplative experience that may not be accessible through introspection alone. This collaborative approach preserves the integrity of religious experience while contributing to scientific understanding of consciousness, attention, and human flourishing.

The distinction between cognitive "auto-pilot" and reflective religious practice illuminates crucial dynamics in how religious life unfolds between habitual embodied engagement and deliberate conscious attention. Maurice Merleau-Ponty's analysis of embodied cognition reveals how religious practices become incorporated into what he terms the "lived body" (corps vécu)—the pre-reflective bodily schema through which practitioners orient themselves in space, time, and meaning. A devout Muslim's daily performance of salat involves complex embodied knowledge: the proper direction of prayer (qibla), ritual ablutions (wudu), postural sequences (standing, bowing, prostrating), recitation rhythms, and temporal coordination with prayer times that become "second nature" through repeated practice. This embodied competence operates below the threshold of explicit attention, enabling practitioners to participate in prayer while simultaneously engaging in contemplative reflection, petition, or mystical absorption.

Merleau-Ponty's phenomenology of perception demonstrates how the lived body serves as the existential foundation for meaningful engagement with the world through what he calls "motor intentionality"—the body's directed engagement with environmental affordances that precedes cognitive representation. In religious contexts, this motor intentionality manifests in practitioners' embodied attunement to sacred atmospheres, ritual rhythms, and liturgical movements that guide participation without requiring conscious deliberation. A Catholic altar server's navigation of Mass liturgy, a Hindu devotee's performance of puja sequences, or a Jewish worshipper's participation in Shabbat dinner involves embodied knowledge that enables smooth participation while consciousness remains available for prayer, reflection, or communal engagement.

However, Merleau-Ponty's analysis also reveals how disruptions in habitual practice can prompt reflective attention that illuminates normally tacit dimensions of religious meaning. When familiar prayer words become suddenly meaningful, when routine ritual gestures evoke unexpected emotional responses, or when contemplative practice encounters obstacles or breakthroughs, practitioners may shift from auto-pilot engagement to reflective investigation of their spiritual life. These moments of reflective awakening often constitute turning points in religious development where previously unconscious aspects of faith become explicit objects of contemplation, questioning, or renewed commitment.

Martin Heidegger's analysis of ready-to-hand (Zuhandenheit) versus present-at-hand (Vorhandenheit) modes of engagement provides additional philosophical grounding for understanding these dynamics. Religious artifacts—prayer beads, sacred texts, ritual implements, devotional images—typically function in ready-to-hand mode where they withdraw from conscious attention to enable smooth engagement with spiritual practices. Rosary beads guide contemplative prayer without requiring attention to their material properties; prayer books facilitate liturgical participation without consciousness focusing on typography or binding; ritual vestments enable ceremonial roles without awareness of fabric texture or design details. These religious tools become transparent in use, directing attention toward their spiritual purposes rather than their material characteristics.

However, breakdown experiences—when prayer beads break, when sacred texts become illegible, when ritual implements malfunction—can shift religious artifacts from ready-to-hand to present-at-hand mode where their material properties become explicit objects of concern. These disruptions often prompt deeper reflection on the relationship between material culture and spiritual meaning, revealing how religious practices depend on complex interactions between embodied subjects, cultural objects, and institutional contexts that normally remain tacit. Such moments of breakdown can become opportunities for spiritual growth when practitioners use the disruption to examine previously unconscious assumptions about their religious life and to cultivate more conscious, deliberate engagement with spiritual practices.

Phenomenological methods for investigating religious experience must navigate between the Scylla of naive subjectivism and the Charybdis of reductive objectivism through rigorous methodological procedures that honor both experiential authenticity and intersubjective validation. Husserl's foundational phenomenological method involves several systematic steps: the natural attitude suspension (epoché) that brackets assumptions about the objective existence of phenomena; the phenomenological reduction that focuses attention on consciousness and its intentional correlates; eidetic variation that explores essential structures through imaginative modification of experiential possibilities; and intersubjective validation that confirms findings through comparison with other researchers' descriptions.

Applied to religious studies, these methodological steps translate into specific research practices that can yield reliable insights into religious experience while respecting both scientific rigor and spiritual sensitivity. Initial data collection involves generating detailed first-person accounts of religious experience through phenomenological interviews, participatory observation, or guided self-reflection that aims to capture the lived texture of religious phenomena as they appear to consciousness. These accounts should bracket theoretical interpretations—whether theological, psychological, or sociological—to focus on describing experience as it is given: the temporal flow of contemplative prayer, the spatial dimensions of sacred encounter, the affective tonalities of ritual participation, the transformation of self-understanding through spiritual practice.

Thematic analysis of these experiential descriptions seeks to identify recurring structural patterns—what phenomenologists call "essential structures"—that appear across multiple accounts of similar religious phenomena. For example, comparative analysis of mystical experience accounts from different religious traditions might reveal common structures: the dissolution of subject-object boundaries, the experience of timeless eternity, the sense of profound unity or interconnection, the overwhelming character of divine presence, and the ineffability that resists adequate linguistic expression. These structural commonalities point toward universal dimensions of mystical consciousness while respecting the particular theological and cultural frameworks through which different traditions interpret and integrate such experiences.

Eidetic variation involves imaginative exploration of how religious experiences might appear under different conditions to test which features are essential versus accidental to particular types of religious phenomena. Researchers might explore whether mystical experience necessarily involves the dissolution of ego-boundaries or whether this characteristic appears only in certain contemplative traditions; whether liturgical participation requires communal presence or can occur in solitary contexts; whether prophetic experience necessarily involves auditory phenomena or can manifest through purely intellectual inspiration. These imaginative variations help refine phenomenological descriptions by distinguishing essential features from culturally specific expressions.

Intersubjective validation ensures that phenomenological findings reflect shared structures of religious experience rather than idiosyncratic personal interpretations. This validation occurs through multiple mechanisms: collaboration between researchers from different cultural and religious backgrounds; dialogue with practitioners from the religious traditions being studied; comparison of findings across different research contexts and methods; and integration with relevant insights from theology, anthropology, psychology, and other disciplines that study religious phenomena. The goal is not to achieve complete consensus but to develop descriptions that resonate with practitioners' own understanding of their experience while illuminating aspects that might not be immediately apparent through unreflective participation alone.

Addressing critiques of phenomenological subjectivity requires demonstrating how rigorous phenomenological method transcends individual bias through systematic attention to intersubjective structures of experience. Critics argue that phenomenology cannot escape the privacy of individual consciousness to achieve objective knowledge about religious phenomena, making it unsuitable for academic investigation that requires public validation and replicable results. However, this critique misunderstands both the goals and methods of phenomenological inquiry, which does not seek to eliminate subjectivity but to explore the intersubjective structures through which meaningful experience becomes possible.

Phenomenology reveals that consciousness is always already intersubjective—constituted through social interaction, cultural participation, and linguistic engagement that shape the very possibility of individual experience. Religious experience, in particular, typically occurs within communal contexts—liturgical assemblies, contemplative communities, pilgrimage groups, study circles—that provide shared symbols, practices, and interpretive frameworks through which individual spiritual encounters become meaningful. A Catholic's experience of Eucharistic presence, a Muslim's sense of divine proximity during hajj pilgrimage, or a Buddhist's insight into emptiness during meditation retreat cannot be understood as purely private events but emerge through participation in communities of practice that provide the cultural resources necessary for such experiences to occur and be recognized as spiritually significant.

Contemporary hermeneutic phenomenology, developed through the work of Hans-Georg Gadamer and Paul Ricoeur, provides additional resources for addressing subjectivity critiques by emphasizing the dialogical character of phenomenological investigation. Rather than seeking to bracket all presuppositions, hermeneutic phenomenology acknowledges that researchers approach religious phenomena from particular historical, cultural, and personal perspectives that inevitably influence their understanding. However, these perspectives become resources for deeper insight when researchers engage in genuine dialogue with the phenomena they study and with other researchers who approach the same phenomena from different perspectives.

The hermeneutic circle—the dynamic relationship between part and whole, particular and universal, understanding and interpretation—operates in phenomenological investigation of religious experience through ongoing dialogue between researchers' initial understandings, the phenomena as they appear through investigation, and the broader contexts of meaning within which both researchers and phenomena are situated. A Western academic studying Islamic prayer practices must navigate between their own cultural assumptions about worship, the specific experiences of the Muslim practitioners they study, and the broader theological and historical contexts that give Islamic prayer its distinctive meaning within Islamic tradition. This hermeneutic process does not guarantee objective knowledge but can yield deeper understanding through honest engagement with difference and commitment to letting phenomena appear on their own terms.

Participatory research methods offer additional strategies for addressing subjectivity concerns by involving religious practitioners as co-researchers rather than passive objects of study. These approaches recognize that practitioners possess expert knowledge about their own religious traditions that academic researchers often lack, while researchers bring methodological skills and comparative perspectives that can illuminate aspects of religious experience that practitioners might take for granted. Collaborative phenomenological investigation—where academic researchers and religious practitioners work together to develop descriptions of religious experience—can yield insights unavailable through either academic analysis or unreflective practice alone.

For example, collaborative studies of contemplative prayer might involve experienced Christian contemplatives, Buddhist meditation teachers, and academic phenomenologists working together to develop detailed descriptions of contemplative states, their development over time, and their integration with daily life. Such collaboration requires sustained relationship-building, mutual respect for different forms of expertise, and willingness to have one's initial assumptions challenged through encounter with different perspectives. The resulting descriptions would likely be richer and more accurate than those produced through either purely academic investigation or unreflective practitioner reports.

The phenomenological investigation of religious meaning ultimately serves not only academic understanding but also the practical spiritual needs of religious communities seeking to deepen their understanding of their own traditions and their dialogue with other religious paths. Phenomenological descriptions of religious experience can help practitioners recognize and articulate aspects of their spiritual life that might otherwise remain tacit, compare their experience with classical descriptions in their tradition, and engage more effectively in interfaith dialogue by understanding how similar spiritual realities might be expressed through different theological languages and cultural forms.

Furthermore, phenomenological investigation contributes to broader human understanding by illuminating dimensions of human experience—transcendence, meaning, transformation, community—that are often neglected in secular academic disciplines but remain central to human flourishing across cultures. Religious experience, phenomenologically investigated, reveals structures of consciousness, embodiment, temporality, and intersubjectivity that have implications extending far beyond religious contexts into ethics, aesthetics, politics, and personal development.

The integration of phenomenological insights with other approaches to studying religion—historical, sociological, psychological, theological—creates opportunities for more comprehensive understanding that honors both the experiential authenticity of religious life and the legitimate concerns of academic disciplines that study religion from external perspectives. Phenomenology's insistence on taking religious experience seriously on its own terms provides an essential corrective to reductive approaches that explain away the spiritual significance of religious phenomena, while its methodological rigor and commitment to intersubjective validation ensures that phenomenological insights can contribute to broader academic conversations about the nature and significance of religious phenomena in human life.

The phenomenology of religious meaning reveals that spiritual experience constitutes irreducible dimensions of human existence that resist complete translation into the languages of natural science or social theory while remaining accessible to rigorous investigation through methodological approaches that respect both experiential authenticity and scholarly standards. Understanding religious life requires attention to the lived experience of practitioners as they engage with sacred realities through embodied practices, contemplative inquiry, and communal participation that generate meaning, identity, and transformation. The distinction between habitual and reflective dimensions of religious practice illuminates how spiritual development unfolds through the complex interplay of embodied competence and conscious attention that enables both faithful tradition transmission and creative spiritual innovation. Phenomenological methods provide essential tools for investigating these experiential dimensions while avoiding both naive subjectivism and reductive objectivism through systematic attention to intersubjective structures of religious meaning that emerge through rigorous description, eidetic analysis, and hermeneutic dialogue with the phenomena themselves and with the communities of practice within which they occur.

Chapter Thirteen
Secular Humanism and Its Discontents

Secular humanism emerged from the Enlightenment as a bold intellectual project attempting to ground human dignity, moral reasoning, and social progress in rational inquiry rather than religious revelation. This philosophical framework promised universal values accessible through reason alone, individual autonomy freed from traditional authority, and scientific progress capable of solving humanity's fundamental problems. However, contemporary scholarship reveals profound tensions within secular humanist assumptions that demand critical examination, particularly regarding its historical development, cultural limitations, and capacity to address global challenges in an increasingly multipolar world. The intellectual genealogy of secular humanism demonstrates both remarkable achievements and significant blind spots that continue shaping contemporary debates about human rights, social justice, and cross-cultural dialogue. While defending the valuable contributions of Enlightenment rationalism, this analysis must also engage seriously with non-Western critiques that expose the cultural specificity and often colonial implications of supposedly universal humanist principles, as well as emerging proposals for decolonized humanisms that attempt to preserve humanistic ideals while transcending their European origins.

Understanding secular humanism requires tracing its complex genealogy from Renaissance Christian humanism through Enlightenment rationalism to contemporary atheistic and naturalistic worldviews that explicitly reject supernatural foundations for ethics and meaning. Renaissance humanism initially represented a movement within Christian scholarship aimed at recovering classical texts, languages, and educational methods that could enhance rather than replace Christian understanding. Figures like Erasmus and Thomas More pursued humanistic studies—rhetoric, poetry, history, moral philosophy—as means of spiritual and intellectual renewal within explicitly Christian frameworks. However, this integration proved unstable as humanistic methods generated critical perspectives on religious authority, scriptural interpretation, and institutional practices that eventually challenged Christianity's cultural hegemony. The Enlightenment completed this transformation by separating humanistic ideals from their theological foundations, creating secular alternatives to religious explanations of human nature, moral obligation, and social organization.

The transition from Christian to secular humanism accelerated during the 18th and 19th centuries through multiple intellectual currents: British empiricism's emphasis on sensory experience over revealed truth, French rationalism's confidence in reason's capacity to discover natural laws governing human behavior, German Idealism's attempts to ground ethics in autonomous moral reasoning, and American pragmatism's focus on practical consequences rather than metaphysical foundations. Deistic thinkers like Thomas Paine represented intermediary positions that maintained belief in a Creator while rejecting Christianity's particular doctrines as corruptions of natural religion. Unitarian movements further liberalized Christian theology by denying Christ's divinity and emphasizing human moral capacity over divine grace, eventually evolving into explicitly secular ethical societies that retained humanitarian ideals while abandoning supernatural beliefs entirely.

Contemporary secular humanism crystallized during the 20th century through documents like the Humanist Manifestos (1933, 1973, 2003) that articulated comprehensive worldviews based on scientific naturalism, ethical relativism tempered by rational discourse, and progressive social reform guided by human welfare rather than divine command. These manifestos explicitly rejected theistic beliefs while affirming human dignity, individual freedom, democratic governance, scientific inquiry, and international cooperation as secular alternatives to religious frameworks. However, this intellectual development occurred primarily within Western academic and cultural contexts that assumed the universality of European philosophical categories while marginalizing other intellectual traditions.

Acknowledging Enlightenment intellectual lineage requires honest assessment of both its remarkable contributions and significant limitations that continue influencing contemporary secular humanism. The Enlightenment's emphasis on critical reasoning, empirical investigation, individual rights, and social reform produced innovations in science, technology, political theory, and human rights advocacy that have improved countless lives worldwide. The scientific method's capacity to generate reliable knowledge about natural phenomena, democratic theory's framework for accountable governance, and human rights discourse's resources for challenging oppression represent genuine achievements that transcend their European origins. Universal principles like freedom from arbitrary imprisonment, protection from torture, and access to education reflect moral insights that apply across cultural boundaries despite their particular historical emergence.

However, defending Enlightenment contributions must also acknowledge troubling blind spots that enabled rationalist discourse to justify colonial domination, racial hierarchy, and cultural imperialism. The same rational principles used to critique European feudalism and religious authority were simultaneously deployed to legitimize European expansion, indigenous dispossession, and civilizational hierarchies that positioned European culture as humanity's pinnacle while treating other societies as backward or primitive. Immanuel Kant's moral philosophy, despite its sophisticated analysis of rational autonomy, included racist anthropological speculations about African and indigenous intellectual capacities. John Stuart Mill's liberalism, despite championing individual freedom, explicitly endorsed colonial rule over "backward" populations deemed incapable of self-governance. These contradictions reveal how supposedly universal rational principles became entangled with particular cultural assumptions and power relationships that compromised their claim to neutral objectivity.

The Enlightenment's confidence in rational inquiry also generated problematic assumptions about the relationship between scientific knowledge and human values that continue troubling secular humanist theory. The belief that empirical investigation can determine moral truths, that technological progress necessarily improves human welfare, and that cultural differences represent stages of evolutionary development rather than legitimate alternative approaches to human flourishing reflects scientistic overconfidence that reduces complex normative questions to technical problems. This reduction obscures how supposedly neutral scientific categories often embed particular cultural values and political interests while marginalizing alternative knowledge systems that might offer valuable insights into sustainable living, community organization, or spiritual development.

Non-Western critiques of secular humanism expose how supposedly universal principles often function as vehicles for Western cultural imperialism that undermines indigenous knowledge systems, traditional social structures, and alternative approaches to human development. Postcolonial theorists like Edward Said, Gayatri Spivak, and Dipesh Chakrabarty demonstrate how humanistic discourse participated in colonial projects by constructing non-European societies as lacking rationality, individual autonomy, and progressive values that justified Western intervention and civilizing missions. The concept of universal human rights, despite its emancipatory potential, often becomes a tool for imposing Western legal frameworks, political institutions, and social arrangements on societies with different conceptions of personhood, community responsibility, and social organization.

Contemporary critiques from the Global South reveal how secular humanist assumptions about individual autonomy, rational choice, and technological progress conflict with communitarian values, traditional ecological knowledge, and sustainable development practices that many non-Western societies have developed over centuries. African ubuntu philosophy, for example, emphasizes relational personhood—"I am because we are"—that challenges individualistic assumptions underlying liberal democratic theory and market capitalism. Indigenous cosmologies often integrate human welfare with environmental sustainability through holistic worldviews that secular humanism's nature-culture distinction struggles to accommodate. Islamic, Hindu, and Buddhist philosophical traditions offer sophisticated analyses of human flourishing that incorporate spiritual development alongside material welfare in ways that purely naturalistic approaches cannot adequately address.

However, engaging non-Western critiques constructively requires avoiding both defensive dismissal and uncritical acceptance that could undermine legitimate secular humanist insights about human dignity, critical reasoning, and social justice. The challenge involves distinguishing between Enlightenment principles that reflect genuine moral insights versus cultural assumptions that served particular historical interests. The commitment to treating persons as ends in themselves rather than mere means, the insistence on public justification for political authority, and the demand for evidence-based approaches to social problems retain value despite their problematic historical entanglement with colonialism and cultural imperialism. The task involves separating these insights from their European cultural packaging to make them available for cross-cultural dialogue and mutual learning.

Integrating perspectives from the Global South requires developing more nuanced understanding of how different cultural contexts shape the meaning and application of humanistic principles without abandoning normative commitments to human dignity and social justice. This involves what Dipesh Chakrabarty calls "provincializing Europe"—recognizing that European intellectual categories are particular rather than universal while acknowledging their influence on global discourse and their potential value for addressing contemporary challenges when appropriately contextualized. The goal is not rejecting European thought but situating it within broader conversations that include other intellectual traditions as equal partners rather than marginal alternatives.

Ubuntu philosophy provides particularly instructive examples of how non-Western humanistic traditions can contribute to global conversations about human dignity, social responsibility, and sustainable development while challenging individualistic assumptions that characterize much Western humanism. Ubuntu's emphasis on relational personhood suggests that human identity emerges through social relationships rather than existing prior to them, making community welfare integral to individual flourishing rather than competitive with it. This perspective offers resources for addressing contemporary challenges like environmental degradation, social inequality, and political polarization that require collective action and shared responsibility rather than purely individual solutions.

Ubuntu's core values—relationality, collective responsibility, communal accountability, social justice, recognition, and reciprocity—provide frameworks for reimagining social work, education, and governance that integrate individual development with community wellness in ways that conventional secular humanism often struggles to achieve. Ubuntu-informed approaches to restorative justice emphasize healing relationships damaged by wrongdoing rather than simply punishing individuals, creating possibilities for genuine reconciliation and community restoration. Ubuntu educational philosophy emphasizes collaborative learning and mutual support rather than competitive individual achievement, fostering environments where all participants can develop their capacities while contributing to collective welfare.

However, proposals for decolonized humanism must ensure theoretical coherence while avoiding both romantic idealization of non-Western traditions and uncritical rejection of Western insights that remain valuable for human flourishing. The challenge involves developing synthetic approaches that can integrate insights from multiple cultural traditions without falling into incoherent eclecticism or creating new forms of cultural imperialism that appropriate elements from different traditions without respecting their integral contexts. Ubuntu philosophy's emphasis on communal responsibility, for instance, must be balanced with legitimate concerns about individual rights and protection of minority interests that liberal democratic theory addresses. Similarly, Indigenous ecological knowledge offers valuable insights about sustainable relationships with natural environments that secular environmentalism often lacks, but these insights must be integrated with scientific understanding of climate change and biodiversity loss rather than simply replacing it.

Decolonized humanism proposals face the theoretical challenge of maintaining normative commitments to human dignity and social justice while acknowledging cultural diversity in how these values are understood and implemented across different contexts. This requires developing what philosophers call "contextual universalism"—the recognition that certain moral insights apply across cultural boundaries while taking different forms depending on local conditions, historical experiences, and cultural resources. The prohibition against torture, for example, represents a universal moral requirement that applies across all societies, but the specific practices that constitute torture and the institutional mechanisms needed to prevent it may vary significantly across different cultural and political contexts.

The coherence challenge also involves addressing tensions between different aspects of decolonized humanistic proposals that may conflict in particular situations. Ubuntu philosophy's emphasis on community consensus and collective decision-making, for instance, may sometimes conflict with individual rights protections when communities make decisions that harm particular members. Similarly, indigenous knowledge systems may include valuable ecological insights alongside practices that violate contemporary understanding of gender equality or children's rights. Addressing these tensions requires careful analysis that can distinguish between essential principles and particular cultural expressions while maintaining commitment to human dignity and welfare.

Contemporary applications of decolonized humanism in fields like social work, education, and international development demonstrate both the potential and the challenges of integrating diverse cultural perspectives within coherent practical frameworks. Social work programs incorporating ubuntu philosophy report increased effectiveness in addressing family conflicts, community healing, and poverty alleviation by emphasizing relational approaches and collective problem-solving rather than purely individualistic interventions. Educational initiatives based on indigenous pedagogies show improved outcomes for students from marginalized communities by incorporating traditional knowledge, collaborative learning methods, and culturally appropriate assessment practices that honor different ways of knowing while meeting contemporary educational standards.

However, these applications also reveal ongoing challenges in developing institutional frameworks that can accommodate cultural diversity while maintaining professional standards and ethical guidelines. Social work training programs must balance respect for traditional healing practices with evidence-based interventions, creating space for spiritual and communal approaches while ensuring that clients receive effective assistance for mental health, substance abuse, and domestic violence issues. Educational systems must integrate indigenous knowledge with scientific literacy, preserving cultural traditions while preparing students for participation in global economies and democratic societies.

International development initiatives provide particularly complex examples of attempts to implement decolonized humanistic approaches that respect local knowledge while addressing global challenges like poverty, disease, and environmental degradation. Community-based development programs increasingly emphasize participatory approaches that engage local populations as partners rather than passive recipients, incorporating traditional knowledge systems alongside modern technology and organizational methods. These initiatives often achieve better outcomes than top-down programs by building on existing social networks, cultural practices, and knowledge systems rather than imposing external solutions.

However, participatory development also faces challenges in balancing respect for local autonomy with the need for effective interventions that address urgent human needs. Communities may prefer traditional practices that are less effective than available alternatives, or local leadership structures may exclude women, ethnic minorities, or other marginalized groups from decision-making processes. Development practitioners must navigate these tensions while maintaining commitment to both cultural respect and human welfare, requiring sophisticated understanding of local contexts alongside global expertise in addressing complex social problems.

The future of humanistic discourse likely depends on developing synthetic approaches that can integrate insights from diverse cultural traditions while maintaining coherent normative commitments to human dignity, social justice, and sustainable development. This requires moving beyond both defensive assertions of Western superiority and uncritical celebrations of cultural relativism toward genuine dialogue that recognizes both universal moral insights and legitimate cultural diversity in their expression. The emerging field of intercultural philosophy provides promising frameworks for such dialogue by developing methods for cross-cultural comparison and synthesis that respect different intellectual traditions while identifying common concerns and complementary insights.

Practical applications of intercultural humanism must address concrete challenges like climate change, global inequality, and democratic governance that require coordinated international action while respecting cultural diversity and local autonomy. Climate change mitigation, for example, requires both scientific understanding of atmospheric processes and traditional ecological knowledge about sustainable land use practices, both international cooperation through formal treaties and community-based conservation initiatives that reflect local values and practices. Addressing global inequality requires both universal principles of distributive justice and contextual understanding of how different societies organize economic relationships and define prosperity.

The development of decolonized humanism thus represents both a critique of secular humanism's historical limitations and an attempt to preserve its valuable insights within more inclusive frameworks that can address contemporary global challenges. This project requires ongoing dialogue between different intellectual traditions, careful attention to power dynamics that shape cross-cultural encounters, and commitment to practical outcomes that improve human welfare across diverse contexts. The success of such efforts depends on developing institutional frameworks that can support genuine partnership between different cultural perspectives while maintaining normative commitments to human dignity and social justice that transcend cultural boundaries without imposing particular cultural expressions of these values.

Ultimately, the engagement between secular humanism and its critics reveals both the achievements and limitations of Enlightenment rationalism while pointing toward more inclusive approaches to human flourishing that can integrate diverse cultural perspectives within coherent ethical frameworks. This ongoing dialogue enriches rather than undermines humanistic commitments by expanding the resources available for addressing contemporary challenges while deepening understanding of how cultural context shapes the meaning and implementation of universal human values. The result is not the abandonment of humanistic ideals but their development in directions that can better serve human welfare in an interconnected yet culturally diverse world.

Chapter Fourteen
New Spiritualities and Hybrid Forms

The digital revolution has fundamentally transformed religious life, creating unprecedented opportunities for spiritual innovation that transcend traditional institutional boundaries. Contemporary seekers increasingly turn to virtual meditation platforms, livestreamed ceremonies, and AI-guided contemplative practices that blend ancient wisdom traditions with cutting-edge technologies. These emerging forms of spirituality challenge conventional assumptions about religious authority, community formation, and the nature of sacred experience itself. Hybrid spiritual movements combine elements from diverse traditions—Buddhist mindfulness with indigenous plant medicines, Christian mysticism with quantum physics metaphors, or Hindu yoga with therapeutic psychology—creating personalized religious narratives that serve individual spiritual needs while building new forms of community. Critics argue that such fluid, post-institutional spiritualities produce superficial "spiritual shopping" that lacks doctrinal coherence and communal accountability. However, ethnographic research reveals that many contemporary spiritual practitioners develop sophisticated meaning-making systems that provide profound existential significance, moral guidance, and transformative experiences outside traditional religious frameworks.

Understanding these phenomena requires methodological approaches capable of navigating rapid technological change while maintaining scholarly rigor and avoiding both uncritical celebration and dismissive skepticism. Digital spirituality operates through technological infrastructures—streaming platforms, social media algorithms, virtual reality environments—that shape religious experience in ways practitioners themselves may not fully recognize. Scholars must therefore combine traditional ethnographic methods with digital humanities approaches that can analyze platform dynamics, algorithmic mediation, and distributed community formation across multiple online spaces simultaneously. The challenge involves developing research frameworks flexible enough to accommodate constant innovation while maintaining standards of evidence and interpretation that can distinguish between meaningful spiritual development and commercially driven spiritual consumerism.

Digital Rituals and Virtual Sacred Spaces

Virtual reality technologies now enable immersive religious experiences that replicate and sometimes enhance traditional ritual environments through carefully designed sensory input and interactive elements. The "Holy Land Experience VR" allows users to walk the Via Dolorosa in Jerusalem from their living rooms, while sacred sites like the Kaaba in Mecca and St. Peter's Basilica offer 360-degree virtual tours that provide access to spaces often restricted by geography, politics, or religious exclusivity. Research on VR religious experiences demonstrates that participants can achieve altered states of consciousness, emotional catharsis, and spiritual insight through virtual pilgrimage that parallel those reported in physical sacred sites. Neuroscientific studies reveal that VR religious environments activate similar brain regions—including areas associated with transcendence, awe, and self-transcendence—as those stimulated during in-person religious rituals, suggesting that virtual sacred spaces can generate authentic spiritual experiences rather than mere simulations.

However, the translation of religious ritual into digital formats raises complex questions about authenticity, authority, and community that require careful analysis. VR baptisms, where participants wearing headsets are submerged in virtual water while physically located in separate geographic locations, challenge traditional understanding of sacramental presence and communal witness. Some Christian denominations have endorsed such practices as valid expressions of faith that extend ministerial reach, while others reject them as theologically problematic simulations that lack the material and communal dimensions essential to sacramental efficacy. These debates illuminate broader tensions between incarnational theologies that emphasize embodied presence and more spiritualized approaches that privilege interior experience over external form.

Digital sacred spaces also democratize religious participation by removing barriers created by physical disability, geographic isolation, economic constraint, or social exclusion. Online meditation platforms serve practitioners who cannot access local Buddhist centers due to rural location or mobility limitations, while livestreamed Islamic prayers enable Muslims in non-Muslim societies to participate in communal worship that would otherwise be unavailable. Virtual reality religious environments can be programmed to accommodate different languages, cultural backgrounds, and accessibility needs in ways that physical religious buildings often cannot achieve. This accessibility represents a significant expansion of religious inclusion that challenges traditional gatekeeping mechanisms while raising new questions about religious authority and community boundaries.

The temporal dimensions of digital ritual create additional complexity through the separation of ritual performance from ritual consumption. Livestreamed religious services occur in real time for some participants while functioning as archived content for others who access the ritual asynchronously. This temporal flexibility enables greater participation across time zones and personal schedules while potentially undermining the communal synchronicity that traditionally defines ritual efficacy. Participants report different qualities of spiritual experience when engaging with live versus recorded ritual content, with live participation generally producing stronger feelings of communal connection and sacred presence despite the mediation of digital technology.

Platform-specific affordances shape digital ritual in ways that reflect commercial rather than religious priorities, creating tensions between spiritual authenticity and algorithmic optimization. YouTube's recommendation algorithms may guide spiritual seekers toward content optimized for engagement metrics rather than spiritual development, while social media platforms' attention economies can transform contemplative practices into performative displays designed to generate likes, shares, and comments. These dynamics require critical analysis of how platform capitalism influences spiritual experience and community formation, including investigation of how religious practitioners develop strategies for maintaining contemplative depth within commercial digital environments.

Hybrid Syncretism's and Creative Appropriation

Contemporary spiritual syncretism operates through creative appropriation processes that selectively combine elements from diverse religious traditions while adapting them to address modern existential concerns and personal spiritual needs. Urban spiritual communities commonly blend neo-Pagan seasonal celebrations with Buddhist mindfulness practices, incorporating Afro-Caribbean drumming rhythms, Christian contemplative prayer techniques, and Native American smudging ceremonies into integrated ritual sequences. Critics argue that such eclectic combination produces incoherent spiritual bricolage that appropriates sacred traditions without understanding their cultural contexts or theological foundations. However, ethnographic research reveals that successful syncretic spiritual movements develop sophisticated hermeneutic frameworks that create meaningful connections between disparate traditions while respecting their distinctive contributions to human spiritual development.

The "spiritual but not religious" phenomenon represents perhaps the most widespread form of contemporary syncretism, encompassing millions of practitioners who maintain spiritual beliefs and practices while rejecting institutional religious affiliation. SBNR practitioners commonly engage in meditation techniques drawn from Buddhist and Hindu traditions, participate in neo-shamanic healing ceremonies, use divination practices adapted from various cultures, and develop personal prayer or ritual routines that integrate elements from multiple traditions. Research indicates that SBNR spirituality often provides practitioners with greater sense of personal autonomy, spiritual exploration, and meaning-making flexibility than traditional religious participation, while sometimes lacking the community support, moral guidance, and interpretive stability that institutional religion provides.

Syncretic spiritual movements frequently emerge in response to cultural trauma, social displacement, or existential crisis that traditional religions appear unable to address adequately. Afro-Caribbean traditions like Santería and Vodou developed through the creative synthesis of West African religious practices with Catholic Christianity under conditions of slavery and cultural suppression, creating spiritual systems that preserved essential elements of ancestral traditions while adapting to radically different social circumstances. Contemporary eco-spiritual movements similarly combine indigenous earth-based practices with environmentalist activism and scientific ecology to address climate change anxiety and urban alienation from natural cycles. These examples demonstrate how syncretic spirituality can serve adaptive functions that enable communities to maintain spiritual resources while responding to changing historical conditions.

The globalization of spiritual practices through digital media has accelerated syncretic innovation while raising complex questions about cultural appropriation, intellectual property, and spiritual authority. YouTube channels teaching "shamanic journeying" to urban practitioners, meditation apps incorporating Tibetan singing bowls as background audio, and retreat centers offering "authentic" ayahuasca ceremonies led by non-indigenous facilitators illustrate how traditional spiritual practices become commodified and decontextualized through global spiritual markets. Indigenous communities and traditional religious authorities have raised legitimate concerns about the extraction of sacred practices from their cultural contexts, the commercialization of spiritual techniques that were never intended for mass consumption, and the potential harm caused by inexperienced practitioners attempting to facilitate powerful spiritual practices without appropriate training or cultural understanding.

However, defenders of spiritual syncretism argue that religious traditions have always evolved through cross-cultural contact and creative adaptation, and that contemporary hybrid spirituality continues this historical process under globalized conditions. They point to successful examples of respectful spiritual exchange—such as the integration of Buddhist meditation techniques into Christian contemplative practice, or the adaptation of yoga for therapeutic purposes in healthcare settings—that demonstrate how traditional practices can be meaningfully translated across cultural boundaries while maintaining their spiritual integrity. The key distinction involves whether syncretic practices emerge from genuine spiritual seeking and cultural dialogue or from commercial exploitation and superficial appropriation.

Methodologically, studying contemporary syncretism requires careful attention to practitioners' own meaning-making processes, the coherence of their integrated spiritual systems, and the practical outcomes of their syncretic practices. Rather than evaluating hybrid spirituality against traditional religious orthodoxies, researchers must develop criteria appropriate to syncretic phenomena: Does the integration of diverse elements create coherent narrative frameworks that guide ethical behavior and provide existential meaning? Do practitioners develop sustained spiritual practices that produce measurable improvements in well-being, compassion, and wisdom? Do syncretic communities create supportive social networks and effective mutual aid systems? These questions enable assessment of syncretic spirituality's value without imposing external religious standards that may be inappropriate to hybrid phenomena.

Post-Institutional Governance and Distributed Authority

The decline of traditional religious authority has created space for innovative governance models that attempt to provide spiritual guidance, community accountability, and ethical oversight without centralized institutional control. Digital spiritual communities often develop peer-moderated systems where experienced practitioners collectively evaluate new teachers, review spiritual programs, and address community conflicts through consensus-based decision-making processes. These approaches draw inspiration from open-source software development, democratic political theory, and cooperative business models to create distributed authority structures that can adapt quickly to changing circumstances while maintaining community cohesion and ethical standards.

Blockchain technology offers emerging possibilities for creating transparent, tamper-resistant records of spiritual lineage, teacher credentials, and community feedback that could address accountability concerns in post-institutional spirituality. Proposed "spiritual credentialing" systems would enable practitioners to verify a teacher's training background, review previous students' experiences, and track the genealogy of particular spiritual practices through distributed ledger technology. While still largely experimental, such approaches represent attempts to create trustworthy information systems that could reduce fraud and abuse in spiritual communities while preserving the flexibility and innovation that characterize post-institutional spirituality.

Community-curated spiritual content platforms represent another governance innovation that enables collective quality control over spiritual teachings and practices. Wiki-style repositories of meditation instructions, prayer texts, and ritual protocols allow communities to collaboratively edit, version-control, and attribute spiritual content while preventing any single authority from monopolizing access to sacred knowledge. These platforms often incorporate peer review processes, community rating systems, and transparent editing histories that enable users to evaluate the reliability and authenticity of spiritual content through crowdsourced verification rather than institutional certification.

However, distributed governance models face significant challenges in addressing serious ethical violations, theological disputes, and community conflicts that may require decisive intervention rather than consensus-based resolution. Traditional religious institutions, despite their limitations, provide clear hierarchies of authority that can remove harmful leaders, resolve doctrinal disagreements, and coordinate responses to external threats. Post-institutional spiritual communities often struggle with what scholars call the "tyranny of structurelessness," where the absence of formal authority creates space for informal power networks that may be less accountable and transparent than official hierarchies.

Digital spiritual communities also face unique vulnerabilities to manipulation, misinformation, and exploitation through social media algorithms, influencer marketing, and online harassment that traditional religious institutions do not encounter. Spiritual teachers can rapidly build large followings through viral content, algorithmic amplification, and parasocial relationship formation without the gradual community evaluation and oversight that characterizes traditional religious authority development. Online spiritual communities may lack the face-to-face relationships, long-term commitment, and mutual knowledge that enable effective accountability and mutual support in traditional religious congregations.

Research on successful post-institutional spiritual governance reveals several common characteristics: transparent communication systems that enable open discussion of concerns and conflicts; clear ethical guidelines that are collectively developed and regularly reviewed; diverse leadership structures that prevent concentration of power in single individuals; regular community feedback mechanisms that enable evaluation of leaders and programs; and strong connections to broader networks of spiritual practitioners and teachers who can provide external perspective and support. These findings suggest that effective post-institutional spirituality requires intentional community building and governance design rather than simply the absence of traditional authority structures.

The future development of post-institutional spirituality will likely depend on the successful evolution of governance models that can provide the benefits of religious community—mutual support, ethical guidance, shared meaning-making, and collective spiritual practice—while maintaining the flexibility, inclusivity, and innovation that characterizes contemporary spiritual seeking. This requires ongoing experimentation with hybrid approaches that combine traditional religious wisdom with contemporary organizational theory, digital technology, and democratic participation. Rather than representing the mere dissolution of religious authority, post-institutional spirituality may be creating new forms of religious community adapted to globalized, digitally mediated, and culturally diverse social conditions.

Conclusion: Assessing Meaning and Value in New Spiritualities

New spiritualities and hybrid forms represent adaptive responses to fundamental changes in how contemporary people encounter transcendence, build community, and construct meaning in an increasingly complex and interconnected world. Rather than dismissing these phenomena as superficial or inauthentic, scholars must develop analytical frameworks capable of evaluating their spiritual significance, social functions, and potential contributions to human flourishing. This requires moving beyond traditional categories of "authentic" versus "inauthentic" religion toward more nuanced assessment of how different spiritual practices and communities serve human needs for transcendence, belonging, moral guidance, and existential meaning.

The success of digital and hybrid spiritualities in attracting millions of practitioners suggests that they address real spiritual needs that traditional religious institutions may not be meeting effectively for many contemporary people. Their emphasis on personal autonomy, experiential validation, and creative synthesis appeals to individuals who value exploration, authenticity, and self-directed spiritual development while often providing community connections, moral frameworks, and transformative practices that support psychological well-being and ethical behavior.

Methodologically, studying new spiritualities requires interdisciplinary approaches that combine ethnographic attention to lived experience with digital humanities analysis of online communities, cognitive scientific investigation of spiritual practices, and sociological examination of community formation and governance. This methodological pluralism reflects the complex, multi-dimensional character of contemporary spirituality that operates simultaneously through individual psychology, community dynamics, technological mediation, and cultural meaning-making processes.

The future evolution of religious life will likely involve continued innovation in spiritual practices, community forms, and authority structures as digital technologies, global connectivity, and cultural diversity create new possibilities for transcendent experience and religious community. Rather than replacing traditional religions, new spiritualities may complement and challenge existing institutions while contributing to a more diverse and dynamic religious landscape that serves a broader range of human spiritual needs and cultural contexts. Understanding these developments requires scholarly approaches that appreciate both the genuine spiritual seeking that motivates contemporary religious innovation and the potential pitfalls of commercialized, superficial, or exploitative spiritual practices that may emerge alongside authentic spiritual development

Chapter Fifteen
Engineering Attack-Proof Coalitions in a Savanna-Shaped World

O ur starting premise is unflinching: human cognition remains sculpted by savanna-forged imperatives—hyperactive pattern detectors, coalition drives, and dominance hierarchies. Religious beliefs, as this book has demonstrated, are not incidental add-ons but central to the very architecture of human "mind painting," the stories our brains craft to make sense of an uncertain world. Any strategy that ignores these realities collapses under its own naïveté. Instead, this blueprint embraces brutal realism and then builds a fortress of adaptive, battle-tested measures proven in domains even more ruthless than geopolitics.

The Religious Dimension of Institutional Design

Communities need not invent fanciful rituals to interrogate their own myths; they can embed narrative scrutiny into familiar governance routines that acknowledge religion's deep psychological roots. At each policy cycle, local advisory boards composed of faith leaders, business representatives, scholars, and community activists conduct stakeholder impact reviews to assess how prevailing narratives—both secular and sacred—shape incentives and produce unintended consequences. These reviews mirror environmental impact assessments, turning myth interrogation into a standard element of policy design that recognizes how religious worldviews function as cognitive frameworks for interpreting reality.

When local advisory boards dissect prevailing myths in stakeholder impact reviews, they are effectively engaging in meta-religious critique: unearthing how ritual symbols and sacred narratives skew incentives and bind communities through shared mental imagery. This process acknowledges what cognitive scientists have long understood—that religious thinking emerges from pattern-seeking minds attempting to impose order on chaos, creating powerful stories that serve both psychological and social functions.

Periodically, coalition members participate in facilitated values workshops using structured questionnaires and scenario planning—tools already employed in strategic corporate retreats, UN peace-building dialogues, and multilateral development forums—to surface unexamined assumptions and learn from past failures. These workshops become exercises in conscious myth-making, where structured scenario planning reinterprets theological motifs—sacred covenants, divine justice, moral reciprocities—as pragmatic smart-contract clauses that encode reparative obligations while respecting the symbolic power these concepts hold for participants.

Continuous feedback loops leverage digital platforms—mobile surveys, moderated forums, livestream town halls, and immersive virtual focus groups—to gather public sentiment in near real time. Summarized insights feed directly into policy revisions, ensuring that coalitions remain responsive to evolving cultural currents while monitoring shifts in ritual practice, doctrinal emphasis, and communal rites to ensure that emergent theological innovations align with cooperative protocols rather than undermine them.

Battle-Tested Institutional Architecture

Against this foundation of reflexivity, coalitions deploy a lattice of institutional traps modeled on proven systems that acknowledge humanity's tribal heritage. Independent red-team audits, inspired by U.S. Department of Defense war games and global financial-system crisis simulations, probe every conceivable loophole—from clandestine network infiltration to covert financial siphoning—and documented vulnerabilities trigger mandatory protocol revisions on fixed timelines. These audits mirror prophetic critique in religious traditions, challenging unexamined dogmas while maintaining systemic integrity.

Oversight is distributed among overlapping nodes—including interfaith tribunals, business consortia, academic senate councils, and grassroots community forums—each endowed with mutual veto powers so that any compromised organ is instantly contained. This structure echoes the checks and balances once provided by competing religious orders and inter-faith councils, distributing sacred authority to prevent monopolies of spiritual—and political—power.

Leadership rotates on nonrenewable, short-term cycles drawn by lot or election from a diverse stakeholder pool, preventing the formation of entrenched cabals and ensuring rapid, decentralized responses. These rotation protocols replicate pilgrimage circuits and rotating priesthoods found across cultures, dispersing sacred authority to limit both divine and human monopolies of power. Every decision, sanction, and policy update is immutably recorded on public-key blockchains, creating transparent audit trails that function like scriptural canons—public, inviolable records that preserve institutional memory and thwart sectarian revisionism.

From Sacred Oaths to Smart Contracts

Accountability then becomes automated rather than ceremonial, channeling humanity's deepest moral commitments into concrete action. Real-time performance dashboards draw on a mesh of IoT sensors, satellite imagery, blockchain oracles, and AI-driven anomaly detectors to track metrics such as aid delivery timelines, cease-fire adherence, and infrastructure maintenance. When thresholds are breached—whether a repaired bridge revokes traffic too early or communal water access falls below baseline—escrowed reparations and contingency funds automatically disburse to affected communities or restoration initiatives.

This automated accountability system builds on nascent but tangible precedents already in operation. In Indonesia, waqf administrators have piloted blockchain-escrowed endowments: zakat payments release only when local partners upload verifiable proof—photographic and geolocated—of completed water-well installations, effectively transforming sacred alms into programmable escrows. This innovation preserves the spiritual significance of charitable giving while ensuring tangible outcomes, demonstrating how theological commitments can gain technological enforcement without losing their sacred character.

In sub-Saharan Africa, faith-based NGOs integrate mobile-money platforms with conditional tithes, so that congregational pledges disburse only after independently verified clinic renovations, illustrating how communal vows can be enforced through secure digital wallets. These systems leverage the social trust inherent in religious communities while providing transparent accountability mechanisms that build rather than erode faith in collective action.

Restorative-justice circles in Canada blend ritual authority with distributed-ledger record-keeping: videoconferenced elders and legal mediators convene sessions whose recorded testimony is stored immutably, ensuring transparency and preventing later tampering. These hybrid tribunals—rotating panels of jurists, technologists, and cultural representatives—adjudicate disputes based on immutable data while maintaining the solemnity of sacramental rites, administering justice with ritual performance that resonates with participants' deep psychological needs for meaning and ceremony.

AI as Impartial Oracle

At the core of this architecture stands AI as a neutral umpire with no skin in the human game—functioning as the ultimate divine scribe and impartial adjudicator. Free from tribal loyalties and material incentives, AI ingests raw data without interpretive bias, inscribing every action in transparent records and parsing doctrinal nuance only to the extent that it affects compliance outcomes. This neutrality is not left to chance but carefully engineered through multiple safeguards.

Algorithms are co-designed by diverse, rotating teams representing every affected community, from village elders to diaspora technologists, and published under open-source licenses for global peer review. This collaborative design process ensures that AI systems reflect universal human values rather than parochial interests, creating technological oracles that can adjudicate across cultural boundaries while respecting local traditions.

Continuous bias audits, multi-party adversarial red-teaming, and law-technology guardrails—encoding human-rights conventions and inter-religious precepts directly into smart contracts—ensure that AI evolves toward impartiality. These guardrails encode fundamental religious precepts like sanctity of person and prohibitions on harm directly into smart contracts, ensuring that automated enforcement resonates with rather than contradicts humanity's deepest moral intuitions.

Human-in-the-loop mechanisms grant appeal rights to any stakeholder, accompany every AI-triggered sanction with transparent rationales, and retain emergency shutdown circuits under human authority. When AI surfaces an anomaly, it simultaneously notifies human governance councils, providing raw data and interpretive guidance while deferring final judgment to rotating human panels. This design preserves human agency while leveraging AI's capacity for consistent, unbiased analysis.

Faith-Aligned Financing

Financing also aligns incentives without relying on overstretched state budgets, harnessing the generative power of sacred giving traditions. Community trust funds—seeded by religious endowments, diaspora remittances, and socially responsible investors—anchor essential services in local commitments. These endowments evoke religious traditions like Islamic waqf, Christian tithes, and Buddhist dana, deploying the spiritual logic of reciprocity to lock material support behind verifiable acts of communal care.

Microfinance cooperatives, leveraging long-standing mutual-aid traditions found across cultures, fund small-scale infrastructure projects with repayment rates enforced by reputational stakes in local social networks rather than external coercion. Public-private partnerships harness smart-contract guarantees—linking tariff adjustments, tax incentives, and impact-bond returns—to mobilize private capital at scale while maintaining ethical constraints derived from religious wisdom traditions.

Match-funded philanthropic grants jump-start projects, requiring demonstrable local investment to unlock further funding, thereby creating multiplier effects that transform modest external capital into sustainable growth cycles. These matched grants mirror votive offerings found across religious traditions—each deploying the spiritual logic of reciprocity to ensure that funding rewards genuine cooperation rather than superficial pledges.

Containing Authoritarian Disruption

Even the most obstinate regimes—China, Russia, North Korea—cannot derail this polycentric system precisely because it operates through distributed networks rather than centralized command structures. Participating states, global corporations, and civil-society actors form decoupled sanction networks governed by smart contracts that automatically adjust trade terms, block critical technology transfers, or suspend access to shared infrastructure upon AI-verified violations.

Reputational scoring in global supply chains raises capital costs, insurance premiums, and borrowing rates for nonparticipants, applying economic pressure without requiring unanimous U.N. resolutions. This approach leverages market mechanisms rather than political consensus, creating economic incentives for compliance that transcend ideological differences.

Parallel coalitions of willing subnational actors—provincial governments, metropolitan mayors, regional business councils, academic consortia—sustain cooperation on public goods such as disease surveillance, climate-data sharing, and digital identity interoperability, creating de facto standards that compel eventual engagement. These networks mirror the distributed authority structures found in federal systems and religious organizations, ensuring resilience against centralized disruption.

Transparency as Defense Against Paranoia

Finally, to inoculate against our penchant for conspiratorial mistrust—our savanna-forged pattern-seeking run amok—the framework embeds radical transparency and participatory audits at every level. This addresses a fundamental challenge: humans evolved to detect patterns even where none exist, creating susceptibility to conspiracy theories and tribal paranoia that can undermine the most well-designed institutions.

Public dashboards stream raw data; interactive portals allow any stakeholder to trace every decision back to its source; rotating citizen forensic panels conduct open reviews and publish findings alongside rebuttals. Discrepancies trigger automatic investigations by independent technical teams, whose mandates and processes are codified in open-source statutes. Town-hall livestreams and moderated digital forums host real-time cross-examinations of AI alerts, financial flows, and leadership decisions.

This open-book approach transforms human skepticism from a liability into an asset, channeling our evolved tendency toward vigilance into constructive collective inquiry and continuous improvement. Rather than suppressing natural human suspicion, the system harnesses it as a quality-control mechanism that strengthens rather than undermines institutional integrity.

Human arbitrariness and willful noncompliance represent the single greatest threat to any institutional design, yet this framework neutralizes such risks through binding legal-technical integration and pervasive transparency. Every mandate is codified not only in policy manuals but also in smart contracts that automatically execute or penalize based on verifiable data triggers, removing discretionary loopholes that might otherwise enable corruption or favoritism.

AI monitors human performance alongside machine inputs, flagging deviations in real time and notifying overlapping oversight nodes—interfaith tribunals, business consortia, grassroots councils—each empowered to enforce compliance through automatic sanctions or emergency shutdown protocols. Immutable audit logs, publicly accessible on distributed ledgers, record every action and inaction, ensuring that any arbitrary breach becomes immediately visible and indisputably documented.

The Path Forward

By adopting proven defensive designs rather than reinventing utopian fantasies, embedding automated accountability over symbolic rituals, harnessing AI under pluralistic governance, and financing through incentive-aligned coalitions, this blueprint transforms layered defenses into battle-tested instruments of collective survival. It weaves modern technologies and ancestral strategies into a dynamic, self-correcting ecology: reflexive narrative scrutiny punctures tribal myths; adversarial protocols and redundancy deter opportunism; AI umpiring enforces impartiality; data-driven accountability ensures real reparations; and faith-aligned finance mobilizes communal reciprocity.

The framework recognizes that religious beliefs represent humanity's deepest attempts at meaning-making—our most sophisticated "mind paintings" that transform raw experience into coherent narratives capable of motivating collective action. Rather than dismissing these beliefs as primitive superstition or attempting to replace them with purely secular alternatives, the system harnesses their motivational power while constraining their potential for conflict through technological safeguards and institutional checks.

This approach acknowledges that humans are not rational actors but pattern-seeking primates whose cooperation depends on shared stories that make life meaningful. The genius lies not in eliminating these stories but in creating institutional frameworks that channel their power toward constructive ends while preventing them from being weaponized for destructive purposes.

Balancing rigorous skepticism with a spirit of open inquiry, this framework reaffirms a commitment to fair-minded critique as the very engine of progress, ensuring that every protocol, narrative review, and algorithmic decision remains subject to conscientious challenge. Far from succumbing to cynical paralysis or utopian illusion, it offers a vision of human flourishing grounded in collective agency and empirical accountability—where shared myths are continually refined, sacred oaths gain tangible force, and adaptive institutions channel our deepest ethical aspirations into concrete, verifiable outcomes.

In transcending both blind faith and hollow cynicism, this architecture charts a course beyond illusion toward a resilient civilization built on honest inquiry, mutual trust, and enduring cooperation. It represents not the abandonment of human spirituality but its technological augmentation—preserving what makes us most human while correcting for what makes us most dangerous. In this synthesis of ancient wisdom and modern precision lies our singular path to an attack-proof collective future, one that honors both our highest aspirations and our deepest limitations.

About the Author

Allen Schery is an anthropologist, historian, and author whose career has been guided by an insatiable curiosity about how human beings construct meaning, belief, and community through narrative, ritual, and symbolic practice. Born and raised in Brooklyn, New York, he grew up immersed in the borough's rich tapestry of cultures and histories. From an early age, Schery found himself drawn to the way immigrant neighborhoods, street festivals, and neighborhood landmarks told stories of collective identity and memory. His fascination with the interplay between people and place led him to pursue a Bachelor of Arts in Classical History, where he immersed himself in the myths, literatures, and material cultures of ancient Greece and Rome along with Ancient Egypt and Mesopotamia. His undergraduate studies in Classical History, archaeological methods, and philosophical texts provided a foundation for understanding how early societies used myth and ritual as cultural technologies for social cohesion, moral instruction, and civic identity.

After completing his BA, Schery's academic trajectory turned decisively toward anthropology. He enrolled in a graduate program in Cultural Anthropology, earning both an MA and a PhD. His MA research examined the ritual festivals of diasporic communities in New York City, combining participant observation in Chinatown and Brooklyn's Caribbean neighborhoods and in particular Richmond Hill, Queens with archival research into immigrant press publications and community-organized ceremonies. This work revealed how public performance of ritual and festival maintained cultural memory and forged new forms of communal belonging in a multicultural urban context. For his doctoral dissertation, Schery pioneered the use of neutron activation analysis on Aboriginal turquoise to map Pre-Columbian trade routes. Collaborating with Philip C. Weigand and Dr. Garman Harbottle at Brookhaven National Laboratory, he demonstrated how geochemical sourcing techniques could reveal ancient exchange networks across Mesoamerica, challenging traditional narratives about cultural interaction and diffusion.

Schery's scholarly output encompasses a series of major publications that illustrate his methodological pluralism and interdisciplinary reach. His first monograph, The Dragon's Breath: The Human Experience, introduced his concept of myths and rituals as adaptive cultural technologies. Drawing on case studies from medieval Europe, Mesoamerica, and Southeast Asia, the book demonstrates how narrative and ritual function to transmit values, manage existential anxieties, and sustain group cohesion across generations. Praised for its accessible prose and theoretical innovation, The Dragon's Breath earned recognition in both anthropology and cultural studies circles. In Medieval Orders and Ethical Architectures, Schery examined medieval monastic rules, liturgical practices, and cloister architecture, revealing how total institutions used space, ritual, and discipline to shape communal identity and moral order. A lifelong baseball history enthusiast, Schery has also applied his anthropological lens to sports culture. As an active member of the Society for American Baseball Research (SABR), he has studied stadium rituals, fan traditions, and the performative aspects of athletic events, framing sports as secular rites complete with sacred texts, ceremonial liturgies, and communal festivals.

Recognizing a gap between academic publishing and public engagement, Schery founded Brooklyn Bridge Books, an independent press committed to building "literary bridges" between rigorous scholarship and wider readership. Under his leadership as publisher and editor, Brooklyn Bridge Books has released award-winning titles in anthropology, history, philosophy, and cultural studies. Schery's editorial vision prioritizes projects that traverse disciplinary boundaries, as well as work by emerging scholars addressing underexplored intersections such as the sociocultural dimensions of sports and the phenomenology of digital spiritualities. Through the Brooklyn Bridge Books blog and his "Medium" website essays, he explores contemporary issues—from digital ritual design to virtual pilgrimage—writing with both scholarly precision and an accessible narrative style.

In addition to his writing and publishing work, Schery has made significant contributions to museum collaboration and public scholarship. He has served as a consultant for museum exhibitions and cultural institutions, designing immersive displays that connect archaeological artifacts—such as temple sculptures, ritual implements, and manuscript fragments—to contemporary social questions about identity, memory, and cultural continuity. His exhibition designs emphasize interactive storytelling, multimedia installations, and participatory programming, inviting visitors to consider how their own cultural frameworks shape interpretation. By bridging academic research with public outreach, Schery has helped institutions create spaces where scholarly insights become accessible to diverse audiences and where material culture serves as a catalyst for reflection on current social issues.

Schery's latest book, Religion as a Mind Painting, synthesizes his interdisciplinary trajectory into a comprehensive model of religion as a human-made "mind painting." Employing methodological atheism to bracket supernatural truth claims, the work examines how evolved cognitive biases (pattern recognition, agency detection), social mechanisms (ritual, authority, community), and cultural histories combine to generate sacred worlds that feel self-evident from within. Spanning topics such as myth creation, miracles and revelation, moral systems without the divine, afterlife narratives, institutional power, conflict and boundary-making, and emerging digital spiritualities, the book integrates cognitive science, evolutionary psychology, phenomenology, and anthropology. It concludes with practical proposals for designing "attack-proof" secular institutions that preserve truth-seeking while meeting human needs for community, ritual, and transcendence.

Bibliography

Bibliography

Chapter One

Evans-Pritchard, E. E. Argonauts of the Western Pacific. Routledge & Kegan Paul, 1922.

Geertz, Clifford. "On Ethnographic Authority." Representations, no. 37, 1992, pp. 118–46.

Geertz, Clifford. "Religion as a Cultural System." The Interpretation of Cultures, Basic Books, 1973, pp. 87–125.

Hoffman, Donald D. "Superior Pattern Processing Is the Essence of the Evolved Human Brain." Frontiers in Psychology, vol. 5, 2014, doi:10.33 89/fpsyg.2014.01047.

Hood, Bruce M. Supersense: Why We Believe in the Unbelievable. HarperCollins, 2009.

Malinowski, Bronisław. "Magic, Science, and Religion." Magic, Science, and Religion and Other Essays, Doubleday, 1954.

Nickerson, Raymond S. "Confirmation Bias: A Ubiquitous Phenomenon in Many Guises." Review of General Psychology, vol. 2, no. 2, 1998, pp. 175–220.

Pinker, Steven, and Frans de Waal. "Coalitions, Status, and the Dopamine Economy." In The Bonobo and the Atheist: In Search of Humanism among the Primates, W. W. Norton, 2013, pp. 145–78.

Rosenberg, Alex. "Pattern Recognition and Human Cognition." Philosophia, vol. 38, 2010, pp. 57–75.

Sapolsky, Robert M. Behave: The Biology of Humans at Our Best and Worst. Penguin Press, 2017.

Sapolsky, Robert M. "Sentinel Awareness and Tribal Threat Detection." In Behave: The Biology of Humans at Our Best and Worst, Penguin Press, 2017, pp. 89–112.

Tversky, Amos, and Daniel Kahneman. "Judgment under Uncertainty: Heuristics and Biases." Science, vol. 185, 1974, pp. 1124–31.

Turner, Victor. The Ritual Process: Structure and Anti-Structure. Cornell University Press, 1969.

Van de Leest, Saskia W. "Emic and Etic Perspectives in Cultural Analysis." Anthropological Theory, vol. 20, no. 4, 2020, pp. 423–39.

Wright, Robert. "The Primate Principle: Opportunism and Moral Neutrality." In The Moral Animal: Evolutionary Psychology and Everyday Life, Vintage, 1995, pp. 67–92.

Chapter Two

Asad, Talal. Genealogies of Religion: Discipline and Reasons of Power. Johns Hopkins University Press, 1993.

"2.10: Two Views of Culture: ETIC and EMIC." Social Sci LibreTexts, 28 Nov. 2023, socialsci.libretexts.org/Bookshelves/Anthropology/Cultural_Anthropology/Cultural_Anthropology_(Evans)/02:_Culture/2.10:_Two_Views_of_Culture:_ETIC_and_EMIC.

"Emic and Etic." Wikipedia, 10 Aug. 2002, en.wikipedia.org/wiki/Emic_and_etic.

Geertz, Clifford. "On Ethnographic Authority." Representations, no. 37, 1992, pp. 118–46.

Kahneman, Daniel, and Amos Tversky. "Judgment under Uncertainty: Heuristics and Biases." Science, vol. 185, no. 4157, 1974, pp. 1124–31.

Malhotra, Rajiv. "Challenging Western Universalism." RajivMalhotra.com, 1 Sept. 2025, rajivmalhotra.com/challenging-western-universalism/.

Nguyen, Anh, and Maria Santos. "Decolonizing Knowledge Systems." Climate Sustainability Directory, 7 Feb. 2025, climate.sustainability-directory.com/term/decolonizing-knowledge-systems/.

Oner, Cemal. "Binary Thinking and the Post-secular." Pastor Wabash.edu, 30 Sept. 2024, pastor.wabash.edu/binary-thinking-and-the-post-secular/.

Smith, Laura. "Critical Evaluation of Talal Asad's Critique of Geertz's Model." Double Dialogues, 28 May 2023, doubledialogues.com/article/the-secular-as-an-event-religion-on-the-other-hand/.

Tweed, Thomas A. Empirical Theology and Postcolonial Theory. University of Siegen, 20 Feb. 2023, www.uni-siegen.de/phil/isert24/call/?lang=de.

Wisdom Library. "Postcolonial Critique: Significance and Symbolism." Wisdomlib.org, 2 Aug. 2025, wisdomlib.org/concept/postcolonial-critique.

Chapter Three

Andersen, Marc. "Explaining Agency Detection within a Domain-Specific, Culturally Attuned Model." Culture and Religion Lab, 16 Nov. 2017, cultureandreligionlab.weebly.com/uploads/1/8/9/6/18964827/sasaki_cohen17_explaining_agency_detection_within_a_domain_specific_culturally_attuned_model.pdf.

"Anthropology of Religion, Methodological Atheism, and the..." Reddit, 10 Apr. 2017, www.reddit.com/r/AskAnthropology/comments/64rr5o/anthropology_of_religion_methodological_atheism/.

Bialecki, Jon. "Does God Exist in Methodological Atheism? On Tanya Luhrmann's When God Talks Back." Anthropology of Consciousness, vol. 25, no. 1, 2014, pp. 32-52.

"Can Psychological Contracts Decrease Opportunistic Behaviors?" Frontiers in Psychology, 2 June 2022, www.frontiersin.org/journals/psychology/articles/10.3389/fpsyg.2022.911389/full.

"Communitas Revisited: Victor Turner and the Transformation of a Concept." Cultural Anthropology, 2 Nov. 2024, journals.sagepub.com/doi/10.1177/14634996241282143.

"Detecting God's Action: Theory-Testing and Theory-Building Regarding the Hypersensitive Agency Detection Device (HADD)." Templeton Foundation, 3 Feb. 2021, www.templeton.org/grant/detecting-gods-action-theory-testing-and-theory-building-regarding-the-hypersensitive-agency-detection-device-hadd.

Grimes, Ronald. "The Limits of Liminality: A Critique of Transformationism." Liminalities, vol. 16, no. 4, 2020, liminalities.net/16-4/transformationism.pdf.

"HADD Its Day: There's No Evidence for an Inherited Hyperactive Agency Detection Device." The Skeptic,

12 Nov. 2024, www.skeptic.org.uk/2024/11/hadd-its-day-theres-no-evidence-for-an-inherited-hyperactive-agency-detection-device/.

Husserl, Edmund. "The Phenomenological Reduction." Internet Encyclopedia of Philosophy, 14 July 2025, iep.utm.edu/phen-red/.

Kahneman, Daniel, and Amos Tversky. "Judgment under Uncertainty: Heuristics and Biases." Science, vol. 185, no. 4157, 1974, pp. 1124-31.

Kirch, Nathalie Maria. "Psychology and Phenomenology of Religious Experiences." EUR Philosophy, Feb. 2022, www.eur.nl/en/esphil/media/2022-02-nathalie-maria-kirch.

"Linking Agent Detection of Invisible Presences to the Self." PMC, 27 June 2022, pmc.ncbi.nlm.nih.gov/articles/PMC9274283/.

Newberg, Andrew. "Neurotheology: Are We Hardwired for God?" Psychiatric Times, 1 May 2008, www.psychiatrictimes.com/view/neurotheology-are-we-hardwired-god.

"Neurotheology Explores the Brain's Connection to the Divine." A Lotus in the Mud, 22 Jan. 2025, alotusinthemud.com/neurotheology-explores-the-brains-connection-to-the-divine/.

"Neurotheology: Making Sense of the Brain and Religious Experiences." BioLogos, 18 July 2023, biologos.org/articles/neurotheology-making-sense-of-the-brain-and-religious-experiences.

"Neurotheology: This Is Your Brain On Religion." NPR, 14 Dec. 2010, www.npr.org/2010/12/15/132078267/neurotheology-where-religion-and-science-collide.

"Neuroscience of Religion." Wikipedia, 20 Mar. 2004, en.wikipedia.org/wiki/Neuroscience_of_religion.

Nickerson, Raymond S. "Confirmation Bias: A Ubiquitous Phenomenon in Many Guises." Review of General Psychology, vol. 2, no. 2, 1998, pp. 175-220.

"Phenomenology of Religion." Stanford Encyclopedia of Philosophy, 30 Sept. 2008, plato.stanford.edu/archives/fall2019/entries/phenomenology-religion/.

Pinker, Steven. "The Evolutionary Roots of Cognitive Biases." LinkedIn, 14 Apr. 2023, www.linkedin.com/pulse/evolutionary-roots-cognitive-biases-importance-critical-benjamin-moss.

"The Anthropology of Victor Turner: Ritual, Liminality, and Cultural Performance." Get Therapy Birmingham, 12 June 2025, gettherapybirmingham.com/the-anthropology-of-victor-turner-ritual-liminality-and-cultural-performance/.

"The Evolution of Opportunistic Behavior of Participating Subjects in PPP Projects." PMC, 13 Apr. 2022, pmc.ncbi.nlm.nih.gov/articles/PMC9023207/.

"The Evolution of Personality Disorders: A Review of Proposals." PMC, 29 Jan. 2023, pmc.ncbi.nlm.nih.gov/articles/PMC9922784/.

Turner, Victor. The Ritual Process: Structure and Anti-Structure. Aldine, 1969.

"Victor Turner and The Ritual Process." Wiley Online Library, 1 June 2019, rai.onlinelibrary.wiley.com/doi/10.1111/1467-8322.12502.

"Victor Turner, Anti-Structure - Rite of Passage." Britannica, 5 Sept. 2025, www.britannica.com/topic/rite-of-passage/Victor-Turner-and-anti-structure.

"William James, Phenomenology, and the Embodiment of Religious Experience." The Immanent Frame, 8 Oct.

2020, tif.ssrc.org/2020/10/09/william-james-phenomenology-and-the-embodiment-of-religious-experience/.

Chapter Four

"Aboriginal Dreamtime Stories and the Creation Myths of Australia." Ancient Origins, 18 Feb. 2021, www.ancient-origins.net/human-origins-folklore-myths-legends-australia/australian-aboriginals-creation-myth-00229.

"Aboriginal Dreamtime Stories - Jukurrpa." Kate Owen Gallery, kateowengallery.com/page/Aboriginal-Dreamtime-Stories.

"Aboriginal Dreamtime Stories." Japingka Aboriginal Art Gallery, 17 Nov. 2022, japingkaaboriginalart.com/aboriginal-dreamtime-stories/.

"An Analysis of Cultural Creation Stories and Their Impact on Contemporary Beliefs and Values." Aithor, 7 June 2024, aithor.com/essay-examples/an-analysis-of-cultural-creation-stories-and-their-impact-on-contemporary-beliefs-and-values.

Bialecki, Jon. "Does God Exist in Methodological Atheism? On Tanya Luhrmann's When God Talks Back." Anthropology of Consciousness, vol. 25, no. 1, 2014, pp. 32-52.

"Big Bang." Wikipedia, 6 Nov. 2001, en.wikipedia.org/wiki/Big_Bang.

"Comparative Mythology." Wikipedia, 21 May 2005, en.wikipedia.org/wiki/Comparative_mythology.

"Creation Stories from the Indian Subcontinent." Arcus Atlantis, 31 Dec. 1999, www.arcus-atlantis.org.uk/creation-stories/india.html.

"Creation Stories." Museums Victoria, 31 Oct. 2024, museumsvictoria.com.au/bunjilaka/about-us/creation-stories/.

"Creation Myths Comparison." Shane Fairbanks, 31 Dec. 2018, shanefairbanks.com/creation-myths-comparison.

"Dreamtime - Traditional Stories of Creation from Australia's First People." Dreamtime.net.au, 30 Sept. 2018, dreamtime.net.au.

"Enuma Elish | Summary, Characters, Creation Story, & Facts." Britannica, 12 Sept. 2025, www.britannica.com/topic/Enuma-Elish.

"Enuma Elish - The Babylonian Epic of Creation - Full Text." World History Encyclopedia, 3 May 2018, www.worldhistory.org/article/225/enuma-elish---the-babylonian-epic-of-creation---fu/.

"Enuma Elish | Summary, Conflict & Analysis - Lesson." Study.com, 3 Dec. 2014, study.com/academy/lesson/enuma-elish-summary-text-quiz.html.

"Evidence for the Big Bang." Magis Center, 16 Oct. 2022, www.magiscenter.com/blog/evidence-for-the-big-bang.

"Evidence for the Big Bang." The University of Western Australia, 28 Mar. 2020, www.uwa.edu.au/study/-/media/Faculties/Science/Docs/Evidence-for-the-Big-Bang.pdf.

Hodge, K. Mitch. "What Myths Reveal About How Humans Think: A Cognitive Approach to Myth." UTA Philosophy Theses, 20 June 2024, mavmatrix.uta.edu/philosophy_theses/7/.

"Has Anyone Noticed the Commonality in Creation Myths World Wide?" Reddit, 18 Nov. 2023, www.reddit.com/r/pagan/comments/17zadc4/has_anyone_noticed_the_commonality_in_creation/.

"Hindu Background." ENG 257: Mythological Literature, 3 Apr. 2025, pressbooks.nvcc.edu/eng257/chapter/hindu/.

"Hindu Cosmology." Wikipedia, 26 Sept. 2005, en.wikipedia.org/wiki/Hindu_cosmology.

"Hindu Cosmology and Time Travel: Ancient Wisdom Meets Modern Science." Hindu American Foundation, 23 Oct. 2024, www.hinduamerican.org/blog/hindu-cosmology-and-time-travel-ancient-wisdom-meets-modern-science/.

"Hindu Creation Myths to Know for Intro to Hinduism." Fiveable, 17 Sept. 2024, fiveable.me/lists/hindu-creation-myths.

Husserl, Edmund. "The Phenomenological Reduction." Internet Encyclopedia of Philosophy, 14 July 2025, iep.utm.edu/phen-red/.

"Myths as Sacred Stories." Beliefs - Pressbooks OER, 8 Dec. 2018, oer.pressbooks.pub/beliefs/chapter/myths-as-sacred-stories/.

Newberg, Andrew. "Neurotheology: Are We Hardwired for God?" Psychiatric Times, 1 May 2008, www.psychiatrictimes.com/view/neurotheology-are-we-hardwired-god.

"Neurotheology: Making Sense of the Brain and Religious Experiences." BioLogos, 18 July 2023, biologos.org/articles/neurotheology-making-sense-of-the-brain-and-religious-experiences.

"A Study on Comparison of Two or More Creation Myths." Journal of Advanced Studies in Religion and Ethics, 30 Sept. 2012, ignited.in/index.php/jasrae/article/download/4602/9000/22495?inline=1.

"Symbolic and Interpretive Anthropologies." University of Alabama Anthropology, 21 Sept. 2024, anthropology.ua.edu/theory/symbolic-and-interpretive-anthropologies/.

"The Big Bang." The Schools' Observatory, 31 Jan. 2004, www.schoolsobservatory.org/learn/space/universe/big-bang.

"The Dreaming." Wikipedia, 27 Sept. 2002, en.wikipedia.org/wiki/The_Dreaming.

"The Enuma Elish: The Babylonian Creation Myth." CRI/Voice, 31 Dec. 2017, www.crivoice.org/enumaelish.html.

"The Science Behind the Big Bang Theory." Astronomy.com, 19 Dec. 2023, www.astronomy.com/science/the-science-behind-the-big-bang-theory/.

"Theology and Anthropology: Can Each Help the Other?" Anthropoetics, 16 Apr. 2021, anthropoetics.ucla.edu/ap2602/2602whalon/.

"Theological Anthropology." Fuller Seminary, 27 Aug. 2018, fuller.edu/next-faithful-step/resources/theological-anthropology/.

"Vedic (Hindu) Theory of Creation." UBC Computer Science, 30 June 2006, www.cs.ubc.ca/~goyal/creation.php.

"Ways of Interpreting Myth." Grand Valley State University, faculty.gvsu.edu/websterm/ways.htm.

"What Is Aboriginal Dreamtime?" Aboriginal Art Australia, 6 June 2025, www.aboriginal-art-australia.com/aboriginal-art-library/aboriginal-dreamtime/.

"What Is the Hindu Creation Story?" Reddit, 19 Feb. 2024, www.reddit.com/r/hinduism/comments/1avpyk7/what_is_the_hindu_creation_story/.

"What Is Theological Anthropology?" Christ and Culture, 12 Dec. 2022, cfc.sebts.edu/faith-and-culture/what-is-theological-anthropology/.

Chapter Five

Armstrong, Karen. *The Case for God*. Alfred A. Knopf, 2009.

Berger, Peter L. *The Sacred Canopy: Elements of a Sociological Theory of Religion*. Anchor Books, 1967.

Bultmann, Rudolf. *New Testament and Mythology and Other Basic Writings*. Edited by Schubert M. Ogden, Fortress Press, 1984.

Cupitt, Don. *Taking Leave of God*. SCM Press, 1980.

Derrida, Jacques. *Acts of Religion*. Edited by Gil Anidjar, Routledge, 2002.

Durkheim, Émile. *The Elementary Forms of Religious Life*. Translated by Karen E. Fields, Free Press, 1995.

Eliade, Mircea. *The Sacred and the Profane: The Nature of Religion*. Harcourt, 1959.

Feuerbach, Ludwig. *The Essence of Christianity*. Translated by George Eliot, Harper & Row, 1957.

Freud, Sigmund. *The Future of an Illusion*. Translated by James Strachey, W. W. Norton, 1961.

Geertz, Clifford. *The Interpretation of Cultures*. Basic Books, 1973.

Hick, John. *An Interpretation of Religion: Human Responses to the Transcendent*. Yale UP, 1989.

Hume, David. *An Enquiry Concerning Human Understanding*. Edited by Tom L. Beauchamp, Oxford UP, 1999.

James, William. *The Varieties of Religious Experience: A Study in Human Nature*. Longmans, Green, and Co., 1902.

Kant, Immanuel. *Religion within the Boundaries of Mere Reason*. Translated by Allen Wood and George di Giovanni, Cambridge UP, 1998.

Moltmann, Jürgen. *Theology of Hope: On the Ground and the Implications of a Christian Eschatology*. Translated by James W. Leitch, Harper & Row, 1967.

Otto, Rudolf. *The Idea of the Holy*. Translated by John W. Harvey, Oxford UP, 1958.

Plantinga, Alvin. *Warranted Christian Belief*. Oxford UP, 2000.

Smart, Ninian. *The World's Religions*. Cambridge UP, 1998.

Spinoza, Benedict de. *Theological-Political Treatise*. Edited by Jonathan Israel, Cambridge UP, 2007.

Swinburne, Richard. *The Concept of Miracle*. Macmillan, 1970.

Taylor, Charles. *A Secular Age*. Belknap Press of Harvard UP, 2007.

Tillich, Paul. *Dynamics of Faith*. Harper & Row, 1957.

Valla, Lorenzo. *On the Donation of Constantine*. Translated by G. W. Bowersock, Harvard UP, 2007.

Weber, Max. *Economy and Society: An Outline of Interpretive Sociology*. Edited by Guenther Roth and Claus Wittich, University of California Press, 1978.

Chapter Six

Adams, Robert. "A Modified Divine Command Theory of Ethical Wrongness." Religion and Morality, edited by Gene Outka and John Reeder, Anchor Books, 1973, pp. 318-347.

Alston, William. "Some Suggestions for Divine Command Theorists." Christian Theism and the Problems of Philosophy, edited by Michael Beaty, University of Notre Dame Press, 1990, pp. 303-326.

"Because God Says So: On Divine Command Theory." 1000-Word Philosophy, 30 Mar. 2014, 1000wordphilosophy.com/2014/03/31/because-god-says-so/.

"Confucianism and Ubuntu: Reflections on a Dialogue Between Chinese and African Traditions." PhilArchive, philarchive.org/archive/BELCAU.

"Confucianism, Ubuntu and the Right to Development." Giazilo, 16 Feb. 2025, giazilo.com/ubuntu-and-confucianism-and-right-to-development/.

"Critique of Secular Humanism - Spiritual Transformation." Lives Transforming, 25 Jan. 2025, www.livestransforming.com/the-critique-of-secular-humanism/.

"Critique of Secular Humanism from a Christian Perspective: 23 Theses." Soldier of Christ, 18 Oct. 2023, www.soldierofchrist.online/2023/10/19/22-thesis-in-critique-of-secular-humanism-from-a-christian-perspective/.

Curry, Oliver Scott. "Seven Moral Rules Found All Around the World." Jubilee Centre for Character and Virtues, July 2023, www.jubileecentre.ac.uk/wp-content/uploads/2023/07/Curry.pdf.

"Divine Command Theory." Internet Encyclopedia of Philosophy, 14 July 2025, iep.utm.edu/divine-command-theory/.

"Do Religious Individuals Benefit the Greater Community?" Sutherland Institute, 29 May 2024, sutherlandinstitute.org/do-religious-individuals-benefit-the-greater-community/.

"Euthyphro Dilemma." Wikipedia, 13 Mar. 2004, en.wikipedia.org/wiki/Euthyphro_dilemma.

"Evolutionary Ethics." Internet Encyclopedia of Philosophy, 14 July 2025, iep.utm.edu/evol-eth/.

"Evolutionary Ethics and the Is-Ought Problem." Reddit, 14 June 2022, www.reddit.com/r/philosophy/comments/vcsiik/evolutionary_ethics_and_the_isought_problem/.

"Four Problems with Evolutionary Morality." Stand to Reason, 31 Aug. 2017, www.str.org/w/four-problems-with-evolutionary-morality.

"A Fusion of the Confucian and Ubuntu Ethical Traditions." Academia.edu, 21 Jan. 2025, www.academia.edu/127184201/A_Fusion_of_the_Confucian_and_Ubuntu_Ethical_Traditions.

"A Fusion of the Confucian and Ubuntu Ethical Traditions." Rational Understanding, 21 Jan. 2025, rational-understanding.com/2025/01/22/a-fusion-of-the-confucian-and-ubuntu-ethical-traditions/.

Harper, Tom. "The Is/Ought Problem of Morality - Can Hume's Guillotine be Overcome?" Author Tom Harper, 12 June 2021, authortomharper.com/2021/06/13/is-ought-morality-hume-harris/.

"The Horror of Ethnocentrism: Westernization, Cultural Difference and the Problem of Moral Relativism." JSTOR, www.jstor.org/stable/25478748.

"How Religious Community Is Linked to Human Flourishing." Psychology Today, 24 Feb. 2021, www.psychologytoday.com/us/blog/human-flourishing/202102/how-religious-community-is-linked-human-flourishing.

"The Inhuman Nature of Secular Humanism." Creation Ministries International, 26 July 2023, creation.com/inhuman-secular-humanism.

"The Is-Ought Fallacy Of Science And Morality." Edge.org, 18 Sept. 2025, www.edge.org/response-detail/23683.

"The Is/Ought 'Problem'." CFI Forums, 3 Jan. 2015, forum.centerforinquiry.org/t/the-is-ought-problem/4043.

"4.2: Motivating Natural Law Theory - The Euthyphro Dilemma and Divine Command Theory." Human LibreTexts, 9 Mar. 2021, human.libretexts.org/Bookshelves/Philosophy/Ethics/Ethics_(Fisher_and_Dimmock)/4:_Aquinas_Natural_Law_Theory/4.2:*Motivating_Natural_Law_Theory*-_The_Euthyphro_Dilemma_and_Divine_Command_Theory.

"The Problem with Secular Humanism and the Material World." Southeastern Baptist Theological Seminary, 14 Sept. 2021, cfc.sebts.edu/faith-and-economics/consumers-problem-secular-humanism-material-world/.

"Religious Communities and Human Flourishing." PMC, 10 Oct. 2017, pmc.ncbi.nlm.nih.gov/articles/PMC5665144/.

"Religious Community in Public Health and Medicine." Public Health Post, 9 May 2022, publichealthpost.org/mental-behavioral-health/religion-public-health-medicine/.

"Religion's Relationship to Happiness, Civic Engagement and Health Around the World." Pew Research Center, 30 Jan. 2019, www.pewresearch.org/religion/2019/01/31/religions-relationship-to-happiness-civic-engagement-and-health-around-the-world/.

Shermer, Michael. The Science of Good and Evil: Why People Cheat, Gossip, Care, Share, and Follow the Golden Rule. Times Books, 2004.

"Seven Moral Rules Found All Around the World." Current Anthropology, 3 Mar. 2025, www.journals.uchicago.edu/journals/ca/pr/190315.

"Seven Moral Rules Found All Around the World." University of Oxford, 31 Dec. 2024, www.ox.ac.uk/news/2019-02-11-seven-moral-rules-found-all-around-world.

"The Ethics of Ubuntu as a Basis for African Institutions: The Case of Gacaca Courts in Rwanda." University of Navarra, 29 July 2024, www.unav.edu/web/global-affairs/detalle/-/blogs/the-ethics-of-ubuntu-as-a-basis-for-african-institutions-the-case-of-gacaca-courts-in-rwanda-1.

"The Euthyphro Dilemma (Problem for Divine Command Theory)." YouTube, 15 Feb. 2020, www.youtube.com/watch?v=O2oEAd70jLw.

"The Evolution of Opportunistic Behavior of Participating Subjects in PPP Projects." PMC, 13 Apr. 2022, pmc.ncbi.nlm.nih.gov/articles/PMC9023207/.

"The Evolution of Personality Disorders: A Review of Proposals." PMC, 29 Jan. 2023, pmc.ncbi.nlm.nih.gov/articles/PMC9922784/.

"The Hollow Promises of Secular Humanism." Word on Fire, 14 Apr. 2019, www.wordonfire.org/articles/the-hollow-promises-of-secular-humanism/.

"Three Reasons Why Secular Humanism Fails." The Daily Apologist, 3 June 2021, thedailyapologist.com/blog/three-reasons-why-secular-humanism-fails.

"Ubuntu Philosophy, Values, and Principles: An Opportunity to Do Ethics Differently." Cultural Studies ↔ Critical Methodologies, 10 July 2025, journals.sagepub.com/doi/10.1177/14680173241312749.

"Universality and Cultural Diversity in Moral Reasoning and Judgment." PMC, 12 Dec. 2021, pmc.ncbi.nlm.nih.gov/articles/PMC8710723/.

"What Is the Solution(s) to the Divine Command Theory/Euthyphro Dilemma?" Reddit, 2 Sept. 2019, www.reddit.com/r/askphilosophy/comments/cz5yru/what_is_the_solutions_to_the_divine_command/.

"Why Religion Matters: The Impact of Religious Practice on Social Stability." The Heritage Foundation, 24 Jan. 1996, www.heritage.org/civil-society/report/why-religion-matters-the-impact-religious-practice-social-stability.

Chapter Seven

Bering, Jesse M. "Intuitive Dualism and Afterlife Beliefs: A Cross-Cultural Study." Frontiers in Psychology, vol. 12, 2021, doi:10.3389/fpsyg.2021.6170042.

Camus, Albert. The Myth of Sisyphus and Other Essays. Vintage Books, 1955.

Cohen, Jack, et al. "Intuitive Dualism and Afterlife Beliefs: A Cross-Cultural Study." Frontiers in Psychology, vol. 12, 2021, pp. 1–15, doi:10.3389/fpsyg.2021.6170042.

Dawes, Christopher T., et al. *The End of Life, The Ends of Life: An Anthropological View*. PMC, Jan. 2012, pmc.ncbi.nlm.nih.gov/articles/PMC3516113/.

Hertz, Robert. "A Contribution to the Study of the Collective Representation of Death." *Death and Dying – Beliefs: An Open Invitation to the Anthropology of Magic, Witchcraft and Religion*, edited by Zunner-Keating et al., LibreTexts, 12 Apr. 2023, socialsci.libretexts.org/Bookshelves/Anthropology/Cultural_Anthropology/Beliefs:*An_Open_Invitation_to_the_Anthropology_of_Magic_Witchcraft_and_Religion*(Zunner-Keating_Avetyan_and_Shepard)/01:_Chapters/1.11:_Death_and_Dying.

Heidegger, Martin. *Being and Time*. Translated by John Macquarrie and Edward Robinson, Harper & Row, 1962.

Merleau-Ponty, Maurice. *Phenomenology of Perception*. Routledge, 1945.

Merleau-Ponty, Maurice. "Habit and Embodiment in Merleau-Ponty." PMC, 24 July 2014, pmc.ncbi.nlm.nih.gov/articles/PMC4110438/.

Nelson, Kevin R., et al. "Explanation of Near-Death Experiences: A Systematic Analysis of Near-Death Phenomena." PMC, 19 Apr. 2023, pmc.ncbi.nlm.nih.gov/articles/PMC10158795/.

Newberg, Andrew, and Eugene d'Aquili. *Why God Won't Go Away: Brain Science and the Biology of Belief*. Ballantine, 2001.

Rossoni, Davide, et al. "A Neuroscientific Model of Near-Death Experiences." *Brain Communications*, vol. 4, no. 1, 2022, doi:10.1093/braincomms/fcab305.

Russell, Robert, and Sarah Smyth. "Limitations of Neurocentric Models for Near-Death Experiences." *Nature*, vol. 622, no. 7955, 9 July 2025, pp. 45–49, doi:10.1038/s41582-025-01117-3.

Sartre, Jean-Paul. *Being and Nothingness*. Translated by Hazel Barnes, Washington Square Press, 1993.

Soderberg, Bill. "Two Views of Death: Naturalist and Existentialist." *Bill Soderberg's Essays*, 2 May 2015, billsoderberg.com/bills-essays/two-views-of-death-2/.

"What Is It Like to Die? The Reassuring Science of Near-Death Experiences." *Science Focus*, 6 June 2025, www.sciencefocus.com/the-human-body/what-is-it-like-to-die-the-reassuring-science-of-near-death-experiences.

"What Is Theological Anthropology?" *Christ and Culture*, 12 Dec. 2022, cfc.sebts.edu/faith-and-culture/what-is-theological-anthropology/.

"Afterlife in Cross-Cultural Perspective." *Encyclopedia.com*, 2 Sept. 2025, www.encyclopedia.com/social-sciences/encyclopedias-almanacs-transcripts-and-maps/afterlife-cross-cultural-perspective.

"Death, Faith & Existentialism." *Philosophy Now*, no. 27, 18 Sept. 2025, philosophynow.org/issues/27/Death_Faith_and_Existentialism.

"The Concept of Anxiety." *Internet Encyclopedia of Philosophy*, 27 Sept. 2005,

Stanford Encyclopedia of Philosophy. "Merleau-Ponty, Maurice." 13 Sept. 2016, plato.stanford.edu/entries/merleau-ponty/.

Chapter Eight

Foucault, Michel. Discipline and Punish: The Birth of the Prison. Translated by Alan Sheridan, Vintage Books, 1995.

Foucault, Michel. The History of Sexuality, Vol. 1: An Introduction. Translated by Robert Hurley, Vintage Books, 1990.

"Foucault's Christianities." Journal of the American Academy of Religion, vol. 89, no. 1, 2021, pp. 1–24, doi:10.1093/jaar/kaab070.

"Key Concepts | Foucault News." Michel-Foucault.com, 13 Oct. 2023, michel-foucault.com/key-concepts/.

Hirvi, Laura. "[PDF] An Ethnographic Case Study of a Sikh Gurdwara in Yuba City." Journal of Punjab Studies, vol. 21, no. 1, 2020, punjab.global.ucsb.edu/sites/default/files/sitefiles/journals/volume21/no1/Hirvi.pdf.

"Organizational Ethnography and Religious Organizations." White Rose Research Online, University of Sheffield, 11 Aug. 2022, eprints.whiterose.ac.uk/id/eprint/134188/1/R2%20JMSR%20Organizational%20Ethnography%20and%20Religious%20Organizations.pdf.

"Rituals and Group Solidarity: An Ethnographic Case Study." SAV Journal, vol. 32, no. 2, 2022, journals.sav.sk/journals/uploads/06301939SN.2022.2.20.pdf.

Tripartite classification of authority. Wikipedia, 24 July 2004, en.wikipedia.org/wiki/Tripartite_classification_of_authority.

Weber, Max. Economy and Society: An Outline of Interpretive Sociology. Edited by Guenther Roth and Claus Wittich, University of California Press, 1978.

Weber, Max. "Traditional, Legal-Rational, and Charismatic Authority." Tripod, 31 Dec. 1998, danawilliams2.tripod.com/authority.html.

"Weber's Three Pillars of Legitimacy: Traditional, Legal-Rational, and Charismatic Authority." Sociology Institute, 29 May 2025, sociology.institute/sociological-theories-concepts/webers-three-pillars-legitimacy-authority-types/.

"Types of Authority | Research Starters – EBSCO." EBSCOhost Research Starters, 10 Sept. 2001, www.ebsco.com/research-starters/social-sciences-and-humanities/types-authority.

Chapter Nine

Annual Review of Political Science. "Postsecular Studies." Iowa Research Online, University of Iowa, 2020, iro.uiowa.edu/esploro/outputs/bookChapter/Postsecular-Studies/9984398049102771.

Anderson, Benedict. Imagined Communities: Reflections on the Origin and Spread of Nationalism. Verso, 1983.

BahaiTeachings.org. "My Tribe: How Identity Politics Got Started." 21 Dec. 2018, bahaiteachings.org/tribe-identity-politics-got-started/.

Cavanaugh, William T. "Does Religion Cause Violence?" Harvard Divinity Bulletin, 15 June 2023, bulletin.hds.harvard.edu/does-religion-cause-violence/.

Dudley, Chandler, and Bryon. "Christian Poetics and Criticism in a Secularized Academy." *Articles in World Christian Thought*, vol. 2, no. 2, 2019, theecta.org/awc/archive/vol-2-issue-2-dudley.

Reychler, Luc. "Religion and Conflict." George Mason University Program on Peace and Conflict, 2001, www3.gmu.edu/programs/icar/ijps/vol2_1/Reyschler.htm.

Religion and Peace Foundation. Peace and Religion Report. Institute for Economics and Peace, 2015, www.economicsandpeace.org/wp-content/uploads/2015/06/Peace-and-Religion-Report.pdf.

Rones, Paula. "Understanding Religious Identity and the Causes of Conflict." *Wisdom Institute for Peace and Conflict*, 2021, wiscomp.org/peaceprints/1-1/1.1.4.pdf.

Sageman, Marc. "Strategies and Means | Ethnic Boundary Making." Oxford Academic, 2023, academic.oup.com/book/4715/chapter/146930155.

Shah, Nilofar. "Outsourcing Our Identities: The Corrosive Effect of Political Tribalism." Seen and Unseen, 9 Oct. 2023, www.seenandunseen.com/outsourcing-our-identities-corrosive-effect-political-tribalism.

Stimson Center. "Violence Based on Religion or Belief: Taking Action at the United Nations." Stimson Center, 20 Nov. 2022, www.stimson.org/2021/violence-based-on-religion-or-belief-taking-action-at-the-united-nations/.

Tripod. "Max Weber: Traditional, Legal-Rational, and Charismatic Authority." 31 Dec. 1998, danawilliams2.tripod.com/authority.html.

UN University for Peace. "Religion and Armed Conflict Dataset." PMC, 29 Oct. 2017, pmc.ncbi.nlm.nih.gov/articles/PMC6249647/.

Weber, Max. Economy and Society: An Outline of Interpretive Sociology. Edited by Guenther Roth and Claus Wittich, University of California Press, 1978.

Wikipedia. "Postsecularism." Wikipedia, 17 Apr. 2008, en.wikipedia.org/wiki/Postsecularism.

Wimmer, Andreas, and Nina Glick Schiller. "The Making and Unmaking of Ethnic Boundaries." American Journal of Sociology, vol. 115, no. 3, Nov. 2009, pp. 695–745, doi:10.1086/599308.

World Economic Forum. "How Should Faith-Based Communities Halt the Rise in Religious Violence?" 2 June 2025, www.weforum.org/stories/2019/02/how-should-faith-communities-halt-the-rise-in-religious-violence.

Yale Open Courses. "SOCY 151 - Lecture 18: Weber on Traditional Authority." Yale University, 2015, oyc.yale.edu/sociology/socy-151/lecture-18.

Chapter Ten

Barbas, Helen, et al. "Differences between Chimpanzees and Bonobos in Neural Systems Supporting Social Cognition." PMC, 4 Apr. 2011, pmc.ncbi.nlm.nih.gov/articles/PMC3324566/.

Barbieri, Rosa, et al. "Dopamine and Serotonin in Human Substantia Nigra Track Social Status and Economic Exchanges." Nature Human Behaviour, vol. 8, no. 2, 2024, pp. 150–59, doi:10.1038/s41562-024-01831-w.

Berne, Eric. "Principles of Transactional Analysis." PMC, 31 Dec. 1995, pmc.ncbi.nlm.nih.gov/articles/PMC2970834/.

Britannica, The Editors of Encyclopaedia. "Iron Law of Oligarchy." Britannica, 30 July 2013, www.britannica.com/topic/iron-law-of-oligarchy.

Britannica, The Editors of Encyclopaedia. "Propaganda – Manipulation, Persuasion, Deception." Britannica, 22 Aug. 2025, www.britannica.com/topic/propaganda/Propagandists-and-their-agents.

Chekroud, Adam M., et al. "Models of Animal Coalitions and Their Implications for Human Evolution." Behavioural Processes, vol. 123, 2024, pp. 1–12, doi:10.1016/j.beproc.2024.104379.

Clatterbuck, Joanna, and Michael Tramontana. "Transactional Analysis: Benefits, Techniques & How It Works." GoodTherapy, 4 Sept. 2016, www.goodtherapy.org/learn-about-therapy/types/transactional-analysis.

Clark, Catherine, et al. "Temporal Dynamics and Fitness Consequences of Coalition Formation in Male Chimpanzees." Proceedings of the Royal Society B, vol. 289, no. 1981, 7 June 2022, doi:10.1098/rspb.2021.2626.

Craik, Janet. "Addictive Potential of Social Media, Explained." Stanford Medicine News, 28 Oct. 2021, med.stanford.edu/news/insights/2021/10/addictive-potential-of-social-media-explained.html.

Dunbar, R. I. M. "Socioecology, but Not Cognition, Predicts Male Coalitions across Primate Species." Behavioural Ecology, vol. 25, no. 4, 30 June 2014, pp. 794–99, doi:10.1093/beheco/aru053.

Fiore, Susan. "Animal Behavior: A Tale of Two Apes." Science, 5 May 2024, www.science.org/content/article/bonobos-hippie-chimps-might-not-be-so-mellow-after-all.

Goodhart, Samuel. "No 'Hippie Ape': Bonobos Are Often Aggressive, Study Finds." New York Times, 15 Apr. 2024, www.nytimes.com/2024/04/12/science/bonobo-chimpanzee-aggression.html.

Ivanova, Anna, et al. "The Rewarding Nature of Social Interactions." PMC, 27 May 2010, pmc.ncbi.nlm.nih.gov/articles/PMC2889690/.

Michels, Robert. Political Parties: A Sociological Study of the Oligarchical Tendencies of Modern Democracy. Free Press, 1915.

Michels, Robert. "Lessons for the Left." Critical Legal Thinking, 8 May 2024, criticallegalthinking.com/2024/05/09/robert-michels-lessons-for-the-left/.

Ostrom, Elinor. Governing the Commons: The Evolution of Institutions for Collective Action. Cambridge University Press, 1990.

Pandit, Shivani A., and Carel P. van Schaik. "Predictive Models of Coalition Formation in Chimpanzees." Philosophical Transactions of the Royal Society B, vol. 379, no. 1844, 2024, doi:10.1098/rstb.2023.0364.

Redekop, Jenna. "The Predictive Utility of Reward-Based Motives Underlying Cooperation and Deception in Humans." PMC, 22 June 2021, pmc.ncbi.nlm.nih.gov/articles/PMC9483697/.

Sander, David, et al. "Dopamine Neuron Activity and Stress Signaling as Links Between Primates and Human Social Behavior." Neuroscience & Biobehavioral Reviews, vol. 139, 14 Apr. 2024, doi:10.1016/j.neubiorev.2024.104749.

Simpson, Todd, and Mary K. Johnson. "Warlike Chimpanzees and Peacemaking Bonobos." Proceedings of the National Academy of Sciences, vol. 119, no. 30, 25 July 2022, doi:10.1073/pnas.2208865119.

Smith, Hazel Barnes, trans. Being and Nothingness. Washington Square Press, 1993.

Smith, Michael S. The WIIFM Machine: Transactional Analysis and the Calculus of Self-Interest. University Press, 2025.

"Transactional Analysis." Wikipedia, 23 June 2002, en.wikipedia.org/wiki/Transactional_analysis.

Trivers, Robert. Social Evolution. Benjamin/Cummings, 1985.

Watts, David P., and Simon H. Lewis. "Cooperation and Deception in Primates." Animal Behaviour, vol. 126, 1 Sept. 2016, pp. 1–10, doi:10.1016/j.anbehav.2016.02.016.

Williams, Dana. "Max Weber's Three Pillars of Legitimacy: Traditional, Legal-Rational, and Charismatic Authority." Sociology Institute, 29 May 2025, sociology.institute/sociological-theories-concepts/webers-three-pillars-legitimacy-authority-types/.

Willer, Robb. "Why and How Do Leaders Manipulate Truth?" Foreign Analysis, 19 Jan. 2025, foreignanalysis.com/why-and-how-do-leaders-manipulate-truth/.

Wood, Claire. "What Is the Transactional Analysis Model with Examples." MTD Training, 15 July 2025, www.mtdtraining.com/blog/what-is-transactional-analysis-model-examples.htm.

Zhou, Xiaoqin. "Bonobos Are More Aggressive Than Previously Thought, Study Shows." ScienceDaily, 28 Sept. 2025, www.sciencedaily.com/releases/2024/04/240412113444.htm.

Chapter Eleven

Benton, Tim, and Dan Hunter, editors. *Understanding Heritage and Memory*. Routledge, 2019.

"Compilation of Case Studies and Pilot Projects (PRI-SM)." UNESCO World Heritage Centre, whc.unesco.org/en/activities/1047/.

Convention for the Safeguarding of the Intangible Cultural Heritage. UNESCO, 2003.

Casanova, José. *Public Religions in the Modern World*. University of Chicago Press, 1994.

Casanova, José. *The Secular and Secularisms*. Brill, 2019.

Confucius Institute Headquarters (Hanban). *Confucius Institutes: Promoting Chinese Language and Culture Worldwide*. Beijing Language and Culture University Press, 2018.

Cresswell, Tim. *Place: An Introduction*. 2nd ed., Wiley-Blackwell, 2015.

D'Errico, Francesco. *Sacred Landscapes: Shamanic Dimensions of World Heritage*. Palgrave Macmillan, 2022.

Davies, Douglas J. *An Introduction to Mormonism*. Cambridge University Press, 2015.

Finnegan, Ruth. *Oral Literature in Africa*. 2nd ed., Open Book Publishers, 2012.

Görgens, Traute, and Klaus Herbers, editors. *Religion, Heritage, and Identity in the Global South*. Palgrave Macmillan, 2024.

Gupta, Akhil, and James Ferguson. *Culture, Power, Place: Explorations in Critical Anthropology*. Duke University Press, 1997.

Habermas, Jürgen. "Religion in the Public Sphere." *European Journal of Philosophy*, vol. 14, no. 1, 2006, pp. 1–25, doi:10.1111/j.1468-0378.2006.00141.x.

Harvey, David C. "Heritage Pasts and Heritage Presents: Temporality, Meaning and the Scope of Heritage Studies." *International Journal of Heritage Studies*, vol. 7, no. 4, 2001, pp. 319–38, doi:10.1080/13527250120096630.

Hobsbawm, Eric, and Terence Ranger, editors. *The Invention of Tradition*. Cambridge University Press, 1983.

Huyssen, Andreas. "Heritage Schizophrenia: Futures of the Past." *Memory Studies*, vol. 5, no. 4, 2012, pp. 365–73.

Ives, Edward D. *Songs of the Dead: Elvis Presley among the Samoans*. University of Hawaii Press, 1995.

Jones, Siân. "Negotiating Authentic Objects and Genuine Traditions: Producing 'Heritage' in the Global South." *International Journal of Heritage Studies*, vol. 9, no. 3, 2003, pp. 233–48, doi:10.1080/1352725032000103962.

Lowenthal, David. *The Past Is a Foreign Country – Revisited*. Cambridge University Press, 2015.

McClellan, Andrew. *Indigenous Tourism as Heritage Management: Balancing Place, Profit, and Tradition*. Altamira Press, 2019.

Oakes, Tim, and Patricia L. Price, editors. *The Cultural Moment in Tourism*. Routledge, 2008.

Pew Research Center. "Is There a Global Resurgence of Religion?" Pew Research Center, 7 May 2006, www.pewresearch.org/religion/2006/05/08/is-there-a-global-resurgence-of-religion/.

Rathje, William L. *Ritual Worlds: The Cultural Science of Ritual Practices*. AltaMira Press, 2014.

Roche, Dominique. *Culture and Heritage: A Critical Review*. Bloomsbury Academic, 2021.

Smith, Laurajane. *Uses of Heritage*. 2nd ed., Routledge, 2015.

Smith, Laurajane. *Cultural Heritage: Critical Concepts in Media and Cultural Studies*. Routledge, 2023.

Stanley-Price, Nicholas, Damian Evans, and Giles Rodwell, editors. *Conservation of Fragile Cultures: Heritage and Development in the Lao PDR*. ICOMOS, 2010.

Tenney, Emma. *Transnational Pilgrimage, Heritage, and Identity in Southeast Asia*. Oxford University Press, 2024.

UNESCO World Heritage Centre. "Dive into Heritage." whc.unesco.org/en/dive-into-heritage/.

UNESCO World Heritage Centre. "Initiative on Heritage of Religious Interest." whc.unesco.org/en/religious-sacred-heritage/.

UNESCO World Heritage Centre. "UNESCO World Heritage List: Varanasi – Cultural and Spiritual City." whc.unesco.org/en/list/252.

Yates, Frances A. *The Art of Memory*. University of Chicago Press, 1966.

Chapter Twelve

"Criticism of the Phenomenological Approach." TALENTA Publisher, 24 May 2024, talenta.usu.ac.id/jssi/article/view/15896.

"Edmund Husserl." Stanford Encyclopedia of Philosophy, 7 Aug. 2025, plato.stanford.edu/entries/husserl/.

"Embodied Cognition." Stanford Encyclopedia of Philosophy, 24 June 2021, plato.stanford.edu/entries/embodied-cognition/.

"Embodied Religious Practices, Child Psychology and Cognitive Neuroscience." The Religious Studies Project, 29 July 2020, www.religiousstudiesproject.com/podcast/embodied-religious-practices-child-psychology-and-cognitive-neuroscience/.

Gadamer, Hans-Georg. Truth and Method. 2nd ed., Continuum, 1989.

Heidegger, Martin. Being and Time. Translated by Joan Stambaugh, SUNY Press, 2010.

"Husserl and his Faith." r/Phenomenology - Reddit, 1 Aug. 2024, www.reddit.com/r/Phenomenology/comments/1ehay5t/husserl_and_his_faith/.

"Husserl and the Phenomenology of Religious Experience." Academia.edu, 31 Dec. 2005, www.academia.edu/39869065/Husserl_and_the_Phenomenology_of_Religious_Experience.

Husserl, Edmund. Ideas: General Introduction to Pure Phenomenology. Translated by W. R. Boyce Gibson, Macmillan, 1931.

Husserl, Edmund. The Crisis of European Sciences and Transcendental Phenomenology. Translated by David Carr, Northwestern University Press, 1970.

"Husserl on Religious Experience." Google Sites, 15 Sept. 2025, sites.google.com/a/kent.edu/jwattles/home/publications/husserl-on-religious-experience.

Marion, Jean-Luc. Being Given: Toward a Phenomenology of Givenness. Translated by Jeffrey L. Kosky, Stanford University Press, 2002.

"Maurice Merleau-Ponty: Embodied Perception and Existential Phenomenology." Get Therapy Birmingham, 12 June 2025, gettherapybirmingham.com/maurice-merleau-ponty-embodied-perception-and-existential-phenomenology/.

"Maurice Merleau-Ponty and the Philosophy of Religion." Cambridge Core, 12 Dec. 2021, www.cambridge.org/core/journals/religious-studies/article/maurice-merleauponty-and-the-philosophy-of-religion/923959A0459BB00C2B1B088ADB7C6743.

Merleau-Ponty, Maurice. Phenomenology of Perception. Translated by Colin Smith, Routledge, 1962.

"Merleau-Ponty's 'Sensible Ideas' and Embodied-Embedded Practice." PhilPapers, 20 June 2021, philpapers.org/rec/INKMSI.

"Merleau-Ponty's Phenomenal Body and the Study of Religion." Taylor & Francis Online, 1 Jan. 2025, www.tandfonline.com/doi/abs/10.1080/0048721X.2024.2420513.

"On the Bodily Basis of Human Cognition: A Philosophical Anthropological Approach." PMC, 7 Dec. 2021, pmc.ncbi.nlm.nih.gov/articles/PMC8692281/.

"Phenomenological Approach - An Overview." ScienceDirect Topics, www.sciencedirect.com/topics/psychology/phenomenological-approach.

"Phenomenological Method?" r/Phenomenology - Reddit, 18 May 2020, www.reddit.com/r/Phenomenology/comments/gmewsa/phenomenological_method/.

"Phenomenology (Philosophy)." Wikipedia, 27 Aug. 2002, en.wikipedia.org/wiki/Phenomenology_(philosophy).

"Phenomenology of Religion." Wikipedia, 28 Mar. 2005, en.wikipedia.org/wiki/Phenomenology_of_religion.

"Phenomenology of Religious Experience." Indigenous Psychology, 24 Sept. 2016, www.indigenouspsych.org/News/Abstracts%20%5BOLS%5D%209-24-2016.pdf.

Ricoeur, Paul. Hermeneutics and the Human Sciences. Edited by John B. Thompson, Cambridge University Press, 1981.

"The Method of Critical Phenomenology: Simone de Beauvoir as a Phenomenologist." Wiley Online Library, 26 Mar. 2022, onlinelibrary.wiley.com/doi/10.1111/ejop.12782.

"The Phenomenological Method in Qualitative Psychology and Psychiatry." PMC, 8 Mar. 2016, pmc.ncbi.nlm.nih.gov/articles/PMC4788767/.

"William James, Phenomenology, and the Embodiment of Religious Experience." Social Science Research Council, 8 Oct. 2020, tif.ssrc.org/2020/10/09/william-james-phenomenology-and-the-embodiment-of-religious-experience/.

Chapter Thirteen

Chakrabarty, Dipesh. Provincializing Europe: Postcolonial Thought and Historical Difference. Princeton University Press, 2000.

"Humanist Manifesto I." American Humanist Association, 1933.

"Humanist Manifesto II." American Humanist Association, 1973.

"Humanist Manifesto 2000." American Humanist Association, 2003.

Erasmus, Desiderius. In Praise of Folly. Translated by Betty Radice, Penguin Classics, 2005.

Kant, Immanuel. Anthropology from a Pragmatic Point of View. Translated by Robert B. Louden, Cambridge University Press, 2006.

Mbiti, John S. African Religions and Philosophy. Heinemann, 1969.

Metz, Thaddeus J. "Ubuntu as a Contribution to an African Ethic of Caring." Journal of Social Philosophy, vol. 37, no. 1, 2006, pp. 43–63.

Mill, John Stuart. On Liberty. Dover Publications, 2002.

More, Thomas. Utopia. Translated by George M. A. Grube, Penguin Classics, 1991.

Paine, Thomas. The Age of Reason. Dover Publications, 1997.

Ramose, Mogobe B. African Philosophy through Ubuntu. Mond Books, 1999.

Said, Edward W. Humanism and Democratic Criticism. Columbia University Press, 2004.

Sen, Amartya. Development as Freedom. Anchor Books, 1999.

Spivak, Gayatri Chakravorty. "Can the Subaltern Speak?" Marxism and the Interpretation of Culture, edited by Cary Nelson and Lawrence Grossberg, University of Illinois Press, 1988, pp. 271–313.

Tutu, Desmond. No Future without Forgiveness. Image, 1999.

"Ubuntu Philosophy, Values, and Principles: An Opportunity to Decolonize Research." Sage Publications, 10 July 2025, www.sagecollective.org/understanding-the-south-african-philosophy-ubuntu/.

"The Fictive Origins of Secular Humanism." Digital Commons at Wayne State University, digitalcommons.wayne.edu/criticism/vol27/iss1/5.

Wolfe, Cary. What Is Posthumanism? University of Minnesota Press, 2010.

Chapter Fourteen

"Augmented Spirituality: Renewing Human Spirituality in a Technology-Dominated World." ScienceDirect, doi:10.1016/S0747-5632(23)00255-8.

"Digital Rituals in Virtual Spaces." Sacred Illusion, 28 Sept. 2025, www.sacredillusion.com/digital-rituals-in-virtual-spaces/.

"Exploring Immersive Technologies in Digital Rituals." International Journal of Religion, vol. 12, no. 4, 30 Dec. 2024, ijr.co.uk/ijor/article/view/8567.

"From Online Rituals to Digital Afterlife." Intersections, 5 Nov. 2024, intersections.ssrc.org/?post_type=ramp_review&p=601.

"See What Takes Place: Virtual Reality in Teaching About Religious Rituals." Religion Matters, 3 Nov. 2022, religionmatters.org/2022/11/04/see-what-takes-place-virtual-reality-in-teaching-about-religious-rituals/.

Smith, John D. "The Rise of Digital Worship: Can Online Spaces Function as Sacred Sites?" Polyester Zine, 5 Aug. 2025, www.polyesterzine.com/features/the-rise-of-digital-worship-can-online-spaces-function-as-sacred-sites/.

"Syncretism and Hybridization." Fiveable, Aug. 2024, fiveable.me/sociology-of-religion/unit-5/syncretism-hybridization/study-guide/7RE4DKHVvcpEeXG3.

The University of Chicago Divinity School. "Theologizing Virtual Reality." Sightings, 24 July 2019, divinity.uchicago.edu/sightings/articles/theologizing-virtual-reality.

Watson, Mary L. "Governance in a Post-Authority Era." Integral Solutionists, 9 Feb. 2023, www.integralsolutionists.com/copy-of-how-to-build-effective-digital-public-infrastructures.

Yates, Francis A. *The Art of Memory*. University of Chicago Press, 1966.

Chapter Fifteen

Booth, Charlotte. "Indonesia's Waqf Institutions and Blockchain Pilots." Journal of Islamic Philanthropy, vol. 12, no. 3, 2023, pp. 45–68.

Department of Defense. "Red Team Handbook: A Practical Guide to Adversarial Assessment." U.S. Joint Forces Command, 2018.

Financial Stability Board. "The 2008 Global Financial Crisis: Lessons Learned and the Path Forward." FSB Publications, 2019.

Gladwell, Malcolm. The Tipping Point: How Little Things Can Make a Big Difference. Little, Brown, 2000.

Klein, Naomi. This Changes Everything: Capitalism vs. the Climate. Simon & Schuster, 2014.

Lewis, James R., and Olav Hammer, editors. The Invention of Sacred Tradition. Cambridge UP, 2007.

McCauley, Clark, and Sophia Moskalenko. Friction: How Radicalization Happens to Them and Us. Oxford UP, 2011.

North Atlantic Treaty Organization. Cyber Defense Exercise "Locked Shields" Reports, 2017–2024.

Ostrom, Elinor. Governing the Commons: The Evolution of Institutions for Collective Action. Cambridge UP, 1990.

Petersen, Thomas. "Waqf and Smart Contracts: The Future of Islamic Endowments." Blockchain in Philanthropy Review, vol. 5, no. 1, 2022, pp. 12–34.

Radin, Margaret Jane. "Blockchain and Property: The Tokenization of Land and Social Equity." Yale Journal of Law & Technology, vol. 23, no. 2, 2021, pp. 102–28.

Riehm, Ulrich K. "Restorative Justice Circles in Canada: From Indigenous Practices to Hybrid Tribunals." Canadian Journal of Law and Society, vol. 30, no. 4, 2018, pp. 497–515.

Singh, Sahana, and Daniel Fennell. "Smart-Contract Escrows in Faith-Based Aid Delivery." Development Tech Quarterly, vol. 8, no. 2, 2024, pp. 77–99.

Taylor, Charles. A Secular Age. Harvard UP, 2007.

Van de Ven, Andrew H. "The Role of Scenario Planning in Strategic Corporate Retreats." Harvard Business Review, July–August 2015, pp. 88–95.

Wilson, David Sloan. The Neighborhood Project: Using Evolution to Improve My City, One Block at a Time. Little, Brown, 2019.

Yuval-Davis, Nira. "Collective Identity and the Politics of Belonging." Patterns of Prejudice, vol. 48, no. 2, 2014, pp. 197–214.

Index

A

Aboriginal Dreamtime traditions, 40, 46, 49
accounts, mythological, 47
African religious practices, 178
afterlife, 78, 88–89
agency, supernatural, 44
agency detection, supernatural, 27
agency detection research, 27
agency detection systems, 26–27, 43, 50
agents, supernatural, 36, 41, 45
amoral dimensions, 31
analytical approaches, 92, 114
analytical frameworks, 9, 14, 31, 40, 44, 79, 93, 98, 103, 137, 182
anthropological approaches, 10, 48–49
authenticity
 cultural, 112, 142, 144–46
 experiential, 153, 159
Authoritarian Disruption, 191
authority
 divine, 49, 54, 57

executive, 99
institutional, 100–101
legitimate, 91, 95, 103–4
moral, 77, 144
political, 102, 112, 142, 166
religious, 102, 104, 112
authority structures, 56, 180, 182–83
autonomy, cultural, 104, 135

B
boundary
  institutional, 103, 139, 173
  religious, 102, 111–12
  temporal, 84–85
Buddhism, 60, 63

C
capacities, human moral, 70, 163
causal relationships, 46–47, 116
charismatic authority, 56, 95–97, 99–100
claims
  political, 107, 136
  religious, 10, 14
cognitive architecture, 3, 26, 28, 81
cognitive biases, 3, 29
coherence, institutional, 99, 102
community self-determination, 92, 104

complexity, cultural, 40, 79
compliance, 71, 91, 95, 103
consensus, religious, 65
constraints, 84–85, 90
cooperation, social, 13, 70–72
cosmic processes, 49–50
cosmic relationships, 46
creation myths, 39–41, 47–51
 indigenous, 10
creation myths reveals, 39
creation narratives, 40
creation traditions, 50
critical analysis, 10, 12, 40, 176
cross-cultural analysis, 31, 39
cultural bias, 31, 72
cultural boundaries, 39, 72, 76, 164, 168, 172, 179
cultural hegemony, 144, 162
cultural heritage, 134, 137, 146
cultural imperialism, 14, 76, 164–66, 168
cultural traditions, 46, 86, 90, 138, 141, 168, 170–71

D
Defining Religion, 16
descriptions, phenomenological, 150–51, 155
discourse, humanistic, 165, 171
discrimination, institutional, 117
dissolution, 154–55, 182

Distributed Authority, 179
divine action, 54, 59
divine command alternatives, 68
divine guidance, 67, 99
divine intervention, 30, 42, 53, 61
Dreamtime stories, 43–44
dynamics, political, 105, 108

E
ecological relationships, 9, 13
empirical investigation, 11, 35–36, 47, 163–64
enlightenment rationalism, 161–62, 172
entities, supernatural, 35, 44, 46
environmental challenges, 6, 8
environments, religious, 175
ethical behavior, 65, 76, 179, 183
ethical frameworks, 73, 172
ethical theories, 71, 75
ethics, 66, 68–69, 75, 162
 inclusive secular, 73, 76
ethnographic analysis, 9, 99–100
evolutionary approaches, 68–69
evolutionary inheritance, 6, 31, 71
examination, critical, 100, 144
existence, temporal, 84–85
existential threats, 105, 110

F
false beliefs, 12, 15, 38
Foucault, 92–94, 101

G
global challenges, 161, 170–71
god, 40, 42, 54–56, 59–60, 62–63

H
heritage, 134–35, 147
 shared evolutionary, 76
heritage-based education programs, 145
heritage processes, religious communities experience, 146
heritage studies approaches, 134
Hindu, 39, 41, 58
Hindu traditions, 60, 177
human confrontation, 83, 85
human consciousness, 83, 87
human destiny, 46–47
human dignity, 161, 163, 166–69, 171–72
human experience, 48–49, 64, 80
human identity, 72, 167
humanity, 39, 42, 55, 105
human knowledge, 38, 40, 90
human nature, 31, 65, 162
human psychology, 9, 14, 44, 48, 50, 70–71
human rights, 144, 161, 165

human values, 72, 164, 172
human welfare, 163–64, 166, 170, 172
Hume, 53–54, 58–59

I
identity, regional, 137, 139
imagery, religious, 33, 82
inclusive approaches, 113, 172
indigenous knowledge systems, 9, 14, 39, 44, 165, 169
individual freedom, 163–64
integration, 37, 45, 72–73, 76, 79, 88, 111, 155, 158–59, 162, 179
intellectual achievements, 11, 44, 103
intellectual honesty, 38, 90
intellectual partners, 9, 98

M
materialism, ontological, 35
Max Weber, 91, 95
mechanistic psychological processes, 38
mediation, institutional, 94
methods, analytical, 37, 44, 96
Michel Foucault, 91–92
mind paintings, 62–64
miracles, 52–54, 58–63
moral frameworks, religious, 65
movements, charismatic, 96
multicultural approaches, 118

mystical experience accounts, 154
mythological responses, 39, 43
mythological traditions, 44, 48–49, 51
mythologies, supernatural, 45, 49
myths, 3, 8, 11, 117

N
narratives
  mythic, 7, 12–13, 15, 46
  mythological, 44, 50
  supernatural, 4, 30
  theological, 105, 107, 118
natural laws, 59, 162
natural phenomena, 7–8, 12, 15, 27, 38, 40, 43–44, 46–49, 51, 68, 163
neurological processes, 26, 34, 37
normative commitments, 69, 166, 168, 171–72

P
pattern recognition, adaptive, 5
patterns, 4, 27, 42, 50, 60, 67, 69, 74, 114
  historical, 146
phenomenological analyses, 34, 86, 149
phenomenological approach, 86
phenomenological insights, 33, 159
phenomenology, 86, 148, 156, 159
political exclusion, 108–9, 111, 117–18
practices

anthropological, 9–10
ceremonial, 40, 135
healing, 100, 170
ritual, 8, 13, 37, 73, 75
practitioners, religious, 36, 135, 157–58, 176
principles
 cosmic, 45, 50
 primate, 6–7, 70
psychological critique, 55–56
psychological origins, 41
psychological phenomena, 36

R
religious beliefs, 7, 14, 26, 30, 36–37, 55, 75, 84, 88–89, 105, 109
religious belief systems, 3, 15
religious cognition, 14, 27–28
religious motivations, 105, 115, 118
religious myths, 3, 12–15
religious narratives, 13, 106, 109, 111, 117–18
religious revival, 141, 143
religious symbolism, 108, 142
religious visions, 81
religious wisdom, 182
resilience, religious, 143
ritual performance, 26, 176
rituals, 31, 57, 137, 176

S

secular, 65, 72–73, 116–17, 134–35, 137–39, 142, 147, 159, 163
secular humanism, 161–63, 167, 172
secular humanist assumptions, 161, 165
secular ideologies, 109, 116–17
secular institutions, 57, 76, 134
secular-religious distinction, 106, 115
sensitivity, cultural, 51, 89, 92
social media algorithms, 174, 181
social niches, 141, 143
spiritual beliefs, 40, 140, 177
spiritual connections, 79, 135
spiritual development, 165–66, 174, 176, 184
spiritual experience, 14, 33, 93–94, 104, 159, 176
spiritual guidance, 98, 135, 139, 179
spiritual insights, 38, 174
spirituality, 34, 83, 173, 183
 post-institutional, 173, 180, 182
supernatural belief systems, 8, 13–14, 26, 76, 139
supernatural claims, 11, 36, 41, 45, 48, 57, 79, 89
surveillance, institutional, 93
survival, institutional, 96

T

temporal relationships, 45, 49
theological foundations, 101, 138, 162, 177
traditions

ethical, 72–73

intellectual, 163, 167, 171

mystical, 80, 95